Also by Leona Turlo Budilovsky

My Mother, Helena

Lady Lee

Leona Turlo Budilovsky

To Marilyn
Leona Budilovsky

iUniverse, Inc.
New York Lincoln Shanghai

Lady Lee

Copyright © 2005 by Leona Budilovsky

All rights reserved. No part of this book may be used or reproduced by any means, graphic, electronic, or mechanical, including photocopying, recording, taping or by any information storage retrieval system without the written permission of the publisher except in the case of brief quotations embodied in critical articles and reviews.

iUniverse books may be ordered through booksellers or by contacting:

iUniverse
2021 Pine Lake Road, Suite 100
Lincoln, NE 68512
www.iuniverse.com
1-800-Authors (1-800-288-4677)

Cover Photo of Johnny and Lee by Suzanne Plunkett

Front cover design by Cindy Szatkowski and Kathie Huddleston

ISBN: 0-595-33361-3 (pbk)
ISBN: 0-595-66865-8 (cloth)

Printed in the United States of America

My daughter Joan, Me, My daughter Jane and My grandchildren, Becky, Richard and Josephine

Dedicated To:

My Daughters

Joan Budilovsky Kuzniar and Jane Zeck

and

My Grandchildren

Richard Zeck, Jr.

Rebecca Zeck

Josephine Budilovsky

and

In Memory of My Son

John "Bud" Budilovsky, Jr.

Contents

Foreword.. xiii
CHAPTER 1 3
CHAPTER 2 8
CHAPTER 3 11
CHAPTER 4 15
CHAPTER 5 19
CHAPTER 6 23
CHAPTER 7 27
CHAPTER 8 33
CHAPTER 9 36
CHAPTER 10 39
CHAPTER 11 43
CHAPTER 12 47
CHAPTER 13 52
CHAPTER 14 57
CHAPTER 15 62
CHAPTER 16 67
CHAPTER 17 74
CHAPTER 18 79

Chapter 19	86
Chapter 20	89
Chapter 21	92
Chapter 22	97
Chapter 23	102
Chapter 24	106
Chapter 25	110
Chapter 26	114
Chapter 27	119
Chapter 28	123
Chapter 29	128
Chapter 30	132
Chapter 31	136
Chapter 32	140
Chapter 33	143
Chapter 34	147
Chapter 35	150
Chapter 36	155
Chapter 37	162
Chapter 38	167
Chapter 39	171
Chapter 40	174
Chapter 41	179
Chapter 42	183
Chapter 43	187

Chapter 44	190
Chapter 45	194
Chapter 46	199
Chapter 47	202
Chapter 48	206
Chapter 49	210
Chapter 50	214

Foreword

Each of us has stories to tell. Most of us begin telling our stories as soon as we are able to. Even as infants, the stories expressed through the twinkle in our eyes beckons the sensitive listener ever closer. As we begin speaking, our stories quickly multiply. The older we get, the more stories to tell.

Leona wasn't always a professional writer, yet she was always a wonderful writer none-the-less. Writing was a way, for example, we worked through our mother/daughter disagreements. We'd write letters to each other after an argument. We'd write out our feelings and leave them in an envelope for the other to read. Perhaps this helped us develop our writing craft—the better we wrote, the quicker we got over disagreements! These letters helped us to know each other more deeply. The spoken word didn't always say the whole story. We found the written word a more expressive way to develop our understanding of each other.

Leona and her mother, my grandmother, were very close. When my grandmother died, Leona's grief was almost overwhelming. To work through the depth of her grief, she wrote stories—stories her mother had told her. These stories evolved into my mother's first published book, **My Mother, Helena**. *At the ripe age of 77, my mother, Leona, became a published author.*

On September 28, 1998, shortly after completing the writing of, My Mother Helena, Leona suffered a massive stroke. Fortunately, she survived. Many months of rehab followed. During this time, she was rarely ever without a pen and paper. She was constantly writing down stories, stories that inspired her and touched her heart. As I read her many stories, they also touched my heart. I encouraged her to write her stories down in a book. I knew that my mother's stories would be an inspiration to others as well—others who may be in rehab, others with stories to tell.

My mother Leona, and I, hope these life stories will inspire you to pick up a pen and paper, and begin writing yours. The twist and turns of your life need not be a hindrance to writing your stories, but rather an inspiration to.

Sincerely,
Joan Budilovsky-Kuzniar
Author and Columnist

Acknowledgements

In the formation and production of this book, I would like to extend my heartfelt appreciation to my daughter, Joan Ann Budilovsky-Kuzniar, an accomplished author of many publications in her own right, for urging me to proceed with the compilation of my book. It takes a lot of effort and energy to write a book such as this. My daughter, Jane, gave me much needed and added moral support—Thank You! My good husband, Johnny, is always there when I need him—Thank You!

Thank you to, Teresa Hoover, for beginning this journey with me in her editorial help and assembly. Thank you to Kathie Huddleston and Chuck Reiter who helped format the pictures in this book. And last but certainly not least...Cindy Szatkowski, my editor, who was always there to assimilate my writings in the proper sequence, design my pictures, inspire my memory, and encourage me along this writing journey making it ever more beautiful—Thank You!

And to all of you (especially my readers) who contributed to the success of my publication, thank you from the bottom of my heart!

Leona Turlo Budilovsky

Me at the age of 22 in 1944

Sometimes, you look at a recipe and see an ingredient that you normally wouldn't cook. Case in point, this recipe has cottage cheese, which we usually eat cold with a wedge of fruit or a bit of jelly. It is in taking the leap and using the ingredient in a new way that you find that breaking out of the norm is sometimes very rewarding. The same is true in life. Sometimes you need to add a new twist to life that will change your way of thinking and acting in order to make it better.

CHEESE ROLLED DUMPLINGS

Ingredients:

1 carton (12 oz.) cottage cheese
6 slices bread
1 teaspoon salt
1/4 lb. butter or margarine
4 eggs
1 cup farina
1/2 cup sugar
1/2 cup bread crumbs

Directions:
Cut bread into small cubes and set aside
Put large pot of water on the stove and bring to boil while mixing other ingredients
Cream butter and add eggs, sugar, salt and cottage cheese with mixer.
Add farina, a little at a time, while continuing to mix.
Add bread cubes and mix in gently with a spoon.
Let mixture stand a short time.

Take a damp linen towel (about 30 inches long) and sprinkle with bread crumbs.
Place the mixture on the towel to form a row near the edge of the long side.
Roll up the towel and tie the short ends with string.
Place in a large pot of boiling water.
Cover and let simmer for 30 minutes.

1

For me, it all began back in the 1940's when life blossomed before me. I was in my twenties and had a passion for dancing. My girlfriends had been asking me to accompany them to different ballrooms in Chicago, but I was shy and didn't know how to dance. I didn't want to get out on the dance floor and make a fool of myself. At times I would ask my brother Ed to practice with me in the living room of our house. While he was always good natured and agreed to help out, he wasn't interested in dancing. He was an excellent athlete and had I asked for help with learning how to throw a football or tackle an opponent, he would've been so very happy to help out as these were the things he excelled at.

My friends would encourage me to go dancing by telling me about the Aragon Ballroom in Chicago. Some ballrooms didn't have as good a reputation as others, but I was assured that the Aragon kept the highest standards. They had a dress and a conduct code. If you did not dress properly, you didn't get in and if you acted poorly once inside, you were taken aside and asked to leave. They further convinced me to go by explaining that there was an hour of lessons on Tuesday nights where new dance steps were taught and practiced.

Everyone wanting to learn new dance steps would form a circle around the dance floor and the head instructor would demonstrate a dance step—whether it was the tango, a waltz or swing. Once we got the basic steps down by copying his movements, he would invite a guy and a gal who were accomplished dancers to come onto the dance floor with him and show how the dance is performed by a couple. These dancers were members of a very select group called the "400 Club" and it was quite an honor to be selected to come forward and demonstrate for the group.

After the demonstration, the "400 Club" members would line up with the men on one side of the room and the ladies on the other and then they would dance with the novices who had come for the lesson. The dance would last for one pass down the length of the dance floor and each person would then go to the back of their respective lines. This would go quickly giving the beginners a chance to dance with several partners.

Often, after the instruction part of the evening I would go upstairs and stand at the balcony railing and just watch as couples danced across the floor. The Aragon was so beautiful with stars twinkling above, a polished dance floor below and a live orchestra playing wonderful music. I so wanted to be the one floating across the floor with everyone watching me. I wanted to feel the magic of letting my body move in time with the beat of the music. It became my mission to learn every dance step and to become the best dancer that I could be.

I loved dancing, but it could be expensive because I would have to pay a cover fee each time I went. At the time, it was $2.50 to get into the Aragon. On top of that were car fare and the cost of a soda or ice cream. It was easy to spend close to $3.00 for the evening or even more if I took a taxi home. I was working at the time, but I always handed my paycheck over to my mother to help with the household bills. She in turn gave me an allowance for car fare and incidentals. Back in the early 40's, I was making about $25 a week. While a quart of milk was about 14¢ and a loaf of bread about 9¢ you can imagine what a big expense it was to dance.

I learned that if I could qualify to be a dance instructress, I wouldn't have to pay the cover fee to get into the Aragon and its sister ballroom, the Trianon. This would be such a great savings for me and I could go dancing more often. I'd practice dancing every chance I could get and soon I was dancing smoothly and confidently as if I'd been born to it. The next time they had tryouts for the "400 Club," I decided to participate.

The 400 Club took its name from a societal club that only allowed entry to the "elite" or "Crème de la crème" of society. Since only the best dancers were accepted into this club, everyone knew that you were accomplished at the craft. My girlfriends and I tried out for this club at the Aragon. We were asked to dance with the head instructor and he'd say whether or not we were good enough dancers to be admitted into this particular club. I danced, passed the test, and was put on the list of instructresses. It was a dream come true!

Being a member of the 400 Club meant I had to be present on Tuesdays at the Aragon or Thursdays at the Trianon so that I could be one of the dancers that gave lessons to the novices. I lived on the North side of Chicago, so I went to the Aragon more often as it was closer to my house. The Trianon was located on the South side of Chicago.

After the lessons, when the ballroom was open to all, the instructors and instructresses lined up on the north side of the ballroom. It was then that anyone who was at the ballroom could chose whoever was at the front of the line to dance with. It was a lot of fun. We not only met new people, but we learned new dance steps as well. Oh, to be young again and to go to the ballroom at least two times a week. We danced, met new people and always talked and laughed a lot with whomever we were with. This was a good time in my life—dancing, dancing and more dancing!

The Aragon's ceiling was two stories high over a huge dance floor and lit to look like a starry night. On the second floor one could sit down, have something to drink or visit. It was open like a balcony so that you could look down at the dance floor and also see the band. It was the perfect vantage point to pick out the good dancers and observe their steps. There was a pipe organ on the second floor that was played during band intermissions that lent to the romantic atmosphere of the place.

As for the music, I liked the bands that played under the direction of Freddy Martin, Wayne King and Dick Jurgens. I especially liked Dick Jurgens who played quite often at the Aragon. Also, I enjoyed listening to Eddie Howard who was the lead vocalist with Jurgens' orchestra. He not only had a terrific voice, but he was a good looking man. In later years he started a band of his own. He did very well with it. Everyone I knew liked his band and his singing.

There was always a large crowd at the ballrooms and everyone was well behaved. If someone was not acting properly, a guard would tap them on their shoulder and ask them to leave the dance floor. The guard would then escort the person to another area and tell them what they were doing that wasn't allowed on the floor. The guards were strict. However, this kept the crowd very well behaved.

The Edgewater Beach Hotel, which was located on the shore of Lake Michigan, on the north side of Chicago, was beginning to feature public dancing several times a week. My girlfriends and I decided to try it and see what the crowd was like. We went there on a warm summer night and found that a dance platform was placed on the sand by the beach with a band on a stage nearby. The atmosphere was charming and beautiful, as was the crowd.

When I went to the dance hall, I not only enjoyed dancing, but I also enjoyed watching others as they danced. Some were very good dancers and I watched as to the steps they did. When I had a partner who was willing to try something new, I'd show him a couple who I thought danced very well and he tried his best to do the same steps they were doing. Many times I was able to follow his lead. I learned new steps this way and became very good at following my partner.

I was a very shy person when I joined the "400 Club." I needed to get over this as I had to dance every week with men I didn't know. As I danced with each man, we talked and I got to know quite a lot about each of them.

While I wanted to get over my shyness, I had no interest in getting married. So many of my girlfriends were getting married and I was seeing the mistakes they were making. I made up my mind I would not get married until the right man came along—even if he didn't come along until I was 80 years old.

My parents - after their reunion in the U.S.

A little bit of vinegar mixed with sugar makes this dish a hit. While life is sometimes acidic like vinegar, we can always hope for the sugar to make it palatable.

OLD FASHIONED COLD SLAW
Ingredients:

1 Large head of Cabbage
1 Spanish Onion
1 Green Pepper (optional)
1 tbsp. Caraway Seed
1 tbsp. Salt
½ tbsp. Pepper
½ to ¾ Cup of Vinegar
1 Cup Sugar
¼ Cup Water.

Shred cabbage then scald with boiling water. Let stand in water for 5 to 10 minutes.
Drain.
Add chopped onion and green pepper, caraway seed, salt, pepper. Set aside.
In sauce pan, bring vinegar, sugar and water to a boil. Pour over cabbage mixture.
Let stand overnight.
Mix again so that cabbage is evenly saturated.
Cover and refrigerate.
Slaw can keep in refrigerator for several weeks.

2

My mother was born in Europe and came to America after she was married. A war was raging in Poland at the time and while my father was able to get one of the last tickets on a ship sailing across the Atlantic, my mother was forced to stay behind in Europe, alone, for another seven years. Their country was involved in World War I and many people were fleeing, making space on ships very difficult to obtain. My mother left her small village and traveled to the big city where she found a job working as a seamstress in a tailor shop. The job included a small room in back of the shop so she was able to make ends meet on a small wage. If it were not for her excellent skills in sewing, I don't know what would have happened to her.

Once the war was over and my mother was able to secure passage to America, my mother had no illusions that life would be easy. In fact, my father had a low paying job and they lived in terrible rented apartments at first. I was the first born child of my parents on March 23, 1922. My brother Ed was the next addition to the family in July of 1923. Two years later in 1925, my mother was blessed with twins, John and Lou.

During their time of separation, my mother experienced many of the atrocities of war. As such, she was very protective of her children and instilled in them a healthy fear of dangerous situations or situations that had the appearance of ending badly. I never wanted my mother to feel fear for me or her other children so when I thought there was danger, I completely removed myself from the situation and I was always firm on my decision.

My mother's parents died during the war. Her only brother never emigrated from Poland. He had a very hard time in Poland during the war. There were times that he hid in the forest for months at a time to avoid being taken away by the military and facing a certain death. He often went without food for long periods of time. The weather wasn't always good, leaving him either wet or cold and he often came home very sick. Because of their experiences with the military in Poland my mother mistrusted this type of authority. Later this affected my mother deeply when my brothers were of age with the coming of World War II.

Our family portrait 1927
Back Row: My mother Helena, My father Ludwik, My cousin Stanley
Middle Row: My twin brothers, John and Lou
Front Row: Me and my brother Ed

Poles were great hunters and often had to fall back on those skills in order to stay alive, especially during times of war. Popular among the dishes in Poland was roast rabbit. My parents loved this dish as it brought them fond memories of home.

ROAST RABBIT ~ Peèený králík
Ingredients:

1 rabbit cut in half
2 strips of bacon, cut into ½" strips
pinch of salt
4–5 cloves garlic, pressed
1 onion, diced finely
1 green pepper, chopped
2 tomatoes, chopped
4 strips of bacon
2½ c water
½ c mushrooms, sliced

If whole, cut a rabbit in half. Slice 2 strips of bacon into small strips, approximately ½" in length. Poke holes randomly into rabbit meat and insert the small strips of bacon into each hole. Rub meat with salt and pressed garlic.

Prepare all vegetables (except mushrooms) and spread them across bottom of a roasting pan. Place rabbit halves on top. Lay 2 strips of bacon on each half and pour in the water. Cover and place in preheated oven.

Cook at 475° F for 1½ hours before removing lid to check liquid levels. If needed, add more water to prevent scorching. Add the sliced mushrooms to the pan around (not atop) rabbit. Return uncovered to oven to brown lightly. Cook another 20 minutes or so but don't let the meat become too dark as it will dry out. Remove the rabbit and serve with red cabbage and dressing.

3

My parents were very thrifty and when I was still a small child, they were able to purchase a house on Magnolia on the North side of Chicago. Even though my parents were really quite poor, the house was very nice. On the first floor were two bedrooms, a kitchen, a dining room and a parlor. In order to afford the mortgage payments, the second floor was rented out to two elderly spinsters. I slept in the bedroom on the first floor across the hall from my parent's room. My brothers, Ed, John and Lou, and Ludwig Turlo—a good family friend from Poland, and my cousin Stanley all slept in the attic.

Our family friend, Ludwig, who we affectionately called Ga, came to America by himself. He had grown up in the same village as my father had in Poland and they were close friends. When he came to America, they quickly agreed that Ga, who was a bachelor and never married, should live with them. It was good to see a face from home.

I have loved my three brothers since the day they were born. Ed who is the closest in age to me was always concerned with my welfare. The twins, Lou and John were born three years after me and were always fun and kind while growing up. All of my brothers were very athletic. Ed was quite a football player and Lou and John distinguished themselves on the golf course.

My father kept rabbits during the depression so we were sure to have meat to eat on Sundays. My mother became a pro at making meals stretch to feed everyone in our household. She would shop at several stores taking advantages of the sales each one was having that week.

Lou and John thought of the rabbits as pets and often went out to the garage to play with them. One week they counted the rabbits and found that one was missing. When dinner was served that Sunday, they put two and two together. They knew the rabbit we were eating was fresh from the garage. They refused to eat it. How could they eat their little pet? Understanding how traumatic this was for my little brothers, my father only sold the rabbits to other families after that and used the money to buy food for our family.

My cousin Stanley came to live with us after his parents were killed in a tragic accident. This was during the depression when our family was at its poorest. My parents welcomed him into our family and always felt as though they had been blessed with another child. There were times when Stanley was difficult, but this was attributable to the tragedy he experienced in his youth.

Ga spent considerable time making the attic very nice for sleeping. There was an outside stairway that led up to the attic so they could all come and go as they pleased. Ga was very lucky and found a job working at Carson Pirie & Scott downtown where he worked as a janitor. He was a reliable worker and this was a good job since he did not speak English well.

Living on Magnolia made my childhood wonderful. I knew that the country was in the midst of a depression and I knew that we never had much money, but our neighbor, Mr. Kaehn made our life rich in so many ways. He was a railroad engineer, was married and had three children, but he was in essence still a child himself.

When he purchased the house next to ours, he also purchased the two adjoining lots that were vacant. He set about creating an imaginary world for his children and their friends. He was an artist and drew beautiful pictures. Even though his talent wasn't good enough to make him famous, he never let a day go by where he wasn't making the neighborhood a prettier place to live.

The empty lots next to his house were at one time decorated in a cowboy theme. The space was used so ingeniously that Chicago newspapers came by to take pictures and write articles for the paper. Everyone was so proud to have such an artist in the neighborhood.

Another thing I remember about him was the old car he had in the garage. I couldn't wait for him to drive the car out of his garage and ask me to go for a ride. I was thrilled to be riding in an automobile. No one in our family knew how to drive a car at that time and there weren't many automobiles around. In fact, he was the only one in the neighborhood to own a car.

In his backyard, he had an above the ground swimming pool which we all found refreshing during hot summer weather—no one had air conditioners back then. The most fun though was his trapeze. I was so young at the time and had no fear of height or of getting hurt. I'd swing through the air hanging on to a thin bar just feeling the happiness and freedom that comes when the air is rushing about you and you are off the ground.

My High School Graduation
1939

Some recipes require a lot of work, but the end result is well worth the effort. It is the same with life, the more work you put into it, the more joy you ultimately reap.

POTATO PANCAKES

Ingredients:

11 Potatoes
Salt
4 Onions
3 Cups of Flour
Garlic Powder
Paprika
1 Tbsp. Kosher Vegetable Soup Mix

Grate potatoes and lightly salt
Finely chop onions and set aside
Pour out any water that has accumulated in the potatoes.
Add onions, flour, garlic powder, paprika and soup mix.
Stir and set aside until ready to fry.

Place lard or oil in frying pan and begin to heat it.
When the lard is hot place 1 tablespoon of the potato mixture into the oil.
Fry until slightly brown.
Turn over and fry another five minutes or so until second side is brown.
When both sides are brown, remove from pan and place on paper towels to absorb grease.

When cooled, they can be eaten.

You'll love them, but be careful when you reach for another and another. They are fattening!!

You can also eat them with applesauce or sour cream.

4

Despite all the fun I was having as a youngster, I often thought about what I wanted to be when I grew up. When I attended the neighborhood Catholic school, I wanted to be a nun and teach. However, when I attended the public school, I decided I wanted to be a just a school teacher and not a nun.

Even so, my very first job was with a company named Rehberger. They made award statues and plaques. I was sixteen years old and worked part time during the school year and full time during the summer. It was a fun job to have. I felt very fortunate to have a job because it was during the time of the Great Depression and many people were out of work. In fact, my father was having a very hard time finding work and my mother began doing laundry in order bring money into the house. I knew that the contribution of my paycheck would help get us through the bad times.

Once the statues or plaques were finished, I would inspect them for flaws then pack them for delivery. The owner of the company would sometimes need me to deliver the finished product. He would give me a streetcar pass and I'd deliver the packages to schools, companies and organizations around Chicago. I got to know the streetcar lines in Chicago very well and felt confident traveling to any place in the city.

When I graduated from high school, I took a full time day job with Montgomery Ward. At night I attended college. I was seventeen when I started working at Montgomery Ward as a packer. Having had prior experience with Rehberger as a packer, I felt well qualified for the job. Merchandise was sent down to me and I'd check the items against the order and then put the items together and either put them in a large envelope or box. I'd protect the items by putting paper in the envelope or box to cushion the items so that they would arrive at the customer's house safely.

After being a packer for several months, the supervisor asked me if I knew how to run an adding machine. I told her I didn't and she told me she'd teach me. She did and I learned quickly. Once I had mastered the adding machine, she told me that she'd try me out as a billing clerk. I was very happy to have the chance for a promotion.

After six months, my supervisor came to me again and expressed how pleased she was with my work and then asked me to take over a new job which was the teaching of new employees as to how to become billing clerks. I still wanted to be a teacher and in fact, for many years I was a trainer when I worked for Montgomery Ward. When new employees were hired, I was told to teach them what they needed to know. This was a respected job. I not only taught the new employees, but also got to know them rather well.

At this time, the country was at war with Korea and many of the men on our staff were leaving to serve their country. With all the new people being hired on, I was very, very busy.

Years later, after I had left Montgomery Ward, I came back one day to visit. It was on this same day that an employee I had known quite well came to visit too. He was a good looking man who had been drafted into the service and he came back from the war with his legs missing. We talked awhile and I honestly felt sorry for him. I think of him from time to time and hope he found a job that would allow him to sit. There were many other men that worked at Wards that I never saw again, and I often wonder what happened to them.

My house at 6714 N. Ashland Avenue in Chicago

I still think of bismarks as ponczki. The wonder of eating something so tasty is associated with the name I first called them. As you will see, our parents influence our lives much more than we think.

PONCZKI (Bismarks)
1 ¼ Cup Milk
½ Cup Sugar
¼ Cup Fat
1 tsp. salt
1 cake of Yeast
½ Cup lukewarm Water
2 Eggs
4 to 5 Cups Flour
Fruit Filling

Scald milk—add sugar, fat and salt. Cool to lukewarm.
Dissolve yeast in lukewarm water. Add to above mixture.
Beat in eggs and add enough water to make a soft dough.
Knead until smooth then place in greased bowl. Brush with fat.
Cover and let rise until doubled in bulk.
Roll out to ¼ inch thick and cut into 2 ½ inch rounds.
Place 1 tsp. of favorite filling in center of one round.
Moisten edge with water and top with 2nd round. Press edges together.
Brush with fat and let rise till double in size.
Deep fry until golden brown on both sides.

5

In 1940, when I was 18 years old my parents moved into a huge two story house with 5 rooms on the first floor and 4 rooms on the second floor. It was located at 6714 North Ashland Avenue in Chicago. The Depression was easing and my parents wanted my brothers, uncle and cousin to have proper bedrooms. There were three bedrooms upstairs, so my brother Ed and my uncle could have their own rooms and my twin brothers would share a room. Downstairs, there were two bedrooms one of which was my parents and one was mine. The house was priced very well for the neighborhood and my parents were happy to have the opportunity to buy it.

My cousin Stanley had gotten married and moved out of the house. The trauma of losing his parents had really taken its toll on him over the years and he was not a man who was at peace with himself. My mother considered him as much one of her own children as we were and endured much anxiety during the years that he lived with us. He was a good person, but spent some time carrying out exploits and at times getting into trouble.

When Stanley got married, he expected his wife to be an idealized version of his mother who cleaned fastidiously and always had dinner waiting for his father when he came home from work. She didn't live up to his expectations and his marriage failed after one year. By this time he was ready to move on with his life and didn't move back in with us.

The house had a large enclosed porch on the front of the house and a small porch overlooking the yard in the back of the house. On hot days I'd enjoy sitting on either the front or back porch. It was a beautiful house and we all enjoyed living in it.

There was a huge guest closet located just north of the parlor in our house. It was just large enough to be a cozy phone booth of our very own. We ordered a phone and had it installed in the closet. My brothers liked this very much because they could talk on the phone with the closet door closed and no one knew who they were talking to. Of course, they were all getting to the age where they were interested in girls, but they didn't want anyone to know they were interested.

There was a fireplace in the parlor. My mother bought artificial logs and placed them in the fireplace. She said this was cleaner than having real logs burning and having to clean up the ashes. While she was rather modern in this aspect, she still held on to tradition in other ways.

My mother never learned more than a few words in English. She insisted that we always speak Polish in her house. In fact, I didn't learn English until I started school when I was 5 years old. My mother thought that if we were proficient in the language of her country we would never lose our past. To this day, I can still speak Polish fluently.

Me in a dress that my mother expertly made for me.

Sometimes life is as sweet as these cookies. In the innocence of youth, I saw men as the sweetness of life...

PRALINE COOKIES
24 Graham Crackers
1 cup butter
1 cup brown sugar
1 cup chopped nuts

Arrange crackers on ungreased jelly roll pan.
Combine butter and sugar in saucepan.
Heat to boiling, stirring constantly.
Boil 2 minutes.
Stir in nuts.
Spoon over crackers.
Bake in 350 degree oven for 10 minutes.
Cut each cracker in half while warm.

Simple and sweet!

6

Whenever I had a special occasion to attend, I'd ask my mother to make a new dress for me. She was an excellent seamstress. We'd start by going to some expensive dress shop and I'd pick a dress or two. The sales lady would bring out my size and I'd try it on. My mother would examine it so she would know how to make it. When we'd get home, I'd draw a picture of the dress and my mother would make a pattern from some old newspaper. We'd then go to the store and buy the material I wanted for the dress. When we got home, my mother would immediately start cutting out the pattern. She'd put the newspaper pattern to me and ask if I wanted it this way or that way. Then she'd cut the material accordingly. She'd baste it and I'd try it on and if it fit and was to my liking, she'd then sew it up on the sewing machine. In no time she'd have it finished and I'd wear it the next time I went dancing. I was so lucky to have a mother who was so willing to make beautiful dresses for me. I had so very many dresses that it was difficult for me to pick the dress I'd wear to whatever function I was going to attend next.

My girlfriends were envious of me because I always had a new dress for every function I attended. In fact, one of my girlfriends asked my mother to make her a dress similar to one I had that she was crazy about. My mother made one for her. My girlfriend loved this dress so very much that she wore it to dances over and over again and was always complimented as to how nice the dress looked on her. She thanked my mother very much. Oh Ma, you were too good to me and my girlfriends too!

One of my favorite dresses was a simple black dress that I dressed up with jewelry. It had a high neck with short cap sleeves and was low wasted with the hem falling just below my knees. It really flattered my figure and I always had fun picking out just the right pieces of jewelry to dress it up.

Every so often, when I had the money, I would buy jewelry for myself. I loved all sorts of colored beads. I would buy necklaces that were long and adorned the dresses my mother made. I often bought matching earrings when they were available. My favorite necklaces had hearts dangling to the bottom.

Now, I had graduated from family parties to ballrooms filled with men wanting to dance and some of them wanted to dance with me. I saw them only as dance partners, not possible boyfriends or husbands. I wasn't ready for that stage of my life. But I did find men attractive and enticing. Frank was one of the first men to steal my heart during the days that I only danced at parties.

Frank was the son of my parent's good friends. He was an excellent dancer. Whenever I was at a friend's party and he was also there, I couldn't help myself—I needed to watch him. He knew so many different steps and always chose a girl who had no problem following him. I wished I could dance as well as he did. He danced with so many different girls and they all followed him beautifully. Oh, so I wished I could dance better than I did and perhaps he would ask me to dance.

In a way, I was in love with Frank. Not as a boyfriend, but as a dance partner. He was tall and handsome and had just the right build to look marvelous on the dance floor. I could imagine what it would be like to follow his lead as his feet barely touched the floor when he danced. Of course his affection for me was that of an older brother. It is perhaps this young girl's crush that led me to my love of dancing.

He began to date a girl who was an excellent dancer and when the two of them went on the floor to dance together, you couldn't help yourself but to watch them. Finally, after some time, he asked his partner to marry him. She accepted right away. They began to plan their wedding. Frank told his intended that he wanted me in the bridal group. She agreed to have me and I was asked and immediately accepted.

She was so in love with him and would do anything he wanted her to do. Her love for him was great and he realized she was the one for him. Their wedding was planned and I went to the church and reception and wished the very best for both of them. From now on, he would only be dancing with one woman. That's the way it should be. And when I decided to get married, I hope it would be just like theirs.

My friend Evelyn having a good time at my party.

*What can I say? There is a time in all our lives when we are down in the dumps…
but when it is because we have been dumped, getting back up can be hard.*

DUMP CAKE
Ingredients:

1 Can (20 oz.) Crushed Pineapple
1 Can Cherry Pie Filling
1 Box Yellow Cake mix
1 Cup chopped Nuts
¼ lb. Margarine

Grease 9" X 13" pan
Pour in pineapple—juice and all. Spread evenly.
Pour in cherry pie filling. Spread evenly.
Sprinkle cake mix over pineapple and cherries.
Sprinkle nuts over cake mix.
Cut margarine into small pieces and distribute evenly.

Bake at 350 degrees for 50 to 55 minutes.

Top with Whipped Cream and serve.

7

A friend was visiting me and we began to talk about fortune telling. She told me that she could teach me if I wanted to learn. Of course, I wanted to learn and so we took out a deck of regular playing cards and she began to explain the meaning of each card. She told me to shuffle the cards and lay them out one by one. After the cards were laid out, she began to tell me what each card meant. I was enraptured with the details. I didn't want to miss a thing. I wrote the meaning of each card down. I began to memorize the meanings and in no time, they were all committed to memory. First, I would shuffle the cards and make believe someone was with me. Then, I would lay the cards out exactly as I was shown. After this, I was ready to read the cards. It wasn't too long before her instructions were complete. I looked forward to the fortune telling mysteries I would soon be revealing to others. I enjoyed this prospect very much!

I soon began to feel I understood the cards rather well and would ask my friends if they wanted their fortunes told. If they did, I'd have them shuffle the cards, lay them out, and read their future. This grew in excitement as more and more of my friends wanted me to read their cards. All I needed was a deck of playing cards.

My best friend Evelyn wanted her cards read. She was in the midst of making plans for her wedding and wanted to know if the future with her betrothed looked good. I had already bought my dress for the wedding. I was to be the maid of honor. Most of her wedding arrangements had already been made. The church had been reserved as well as a hall for dinner after the ceremony. The invitations were printed, the cake ordered and all the people standing up for the wedding were selected. I still needed to buy shoes to match my dress, but Evelyn had her complete wedding trousseau ready. Her fiancée had gone to California before the wedding to visit his parents and she was missing him terribly.

I laid the cards out on the table and began to read the message. Now, up to this point, I didn't take all this very seriously. It was just a fun game to play and see if anything really came true. When I read the cards I was a bit flabbergasted, but continued on to tell her what they said. I told her that her intended was dating a girl he met in California and he was getting serious with her. She didn't want to believe me, however, a few days later she got a call from him and he told her he was going to marry a girl he met in California. He told her he couldn't help it, but they fell in love and would be getting married in a few weeks. He said they would have gotten married sooner, but the church was not available for several more weeks.

Of course, Evelyn called me right away and she was beside herself. I must say that I felt very bad. After that, I didn't have any desire to go on reading cards for my friends. It was supposed to be a silly game—not a predictor of bad things to come.

Evelyn felt very bad. How could he do this to her? She could not get out of bed and go to work for weeks. She was so depressed. If anyone asked her about it, she would burst out crying. She felt so humiliated and alone. At least he would stay in California and she would not have to worry about bumping into him on the street.

I decided to have a party at my house to try to lift her spirits. My mother told me that she would make dinner for all my lady friends if I wanted. My mother was a great cook and I knew my friends would love to come for dinner. I invited all of our girl friends over and we did have a great time. My mother made a delicious meal and after it was over, I asked everyone to come downstairs to our basement.

I had a record player and so we put that on and sang along to the hits of the day. We enjoyed that. One of us had a camera and we started taking pictures of each other pretending to be "bad" girls. In one picture, a friend held an empty beer bottle, in another a friend held an unlit cigarette. Then Evelyn took a flower, held it between her teeth, and began dancing a rumba. We all fell over laughing. We ate, listened to music, teased each other and had a wonderful time. It seemed to perk Evelyn up a bit and I was glad we did it.

When word got out that Evelyn's wedding had been cancelled, her fiancé's best friend came over to visit her. He always had a thing for Evelyn, but never pursued it because she was dating his best friend. Now that it was over, he saw this as his chance to get to know her better. He asked Evelyn to go out with him. She liked him and accepted the offer. They went out to dinner together and talked and talked. She found that he was a very interesting person and was pleased that he was spending time with her.

The local church was having a dance and he asked her to go with him. She accepted the offer of this second date and they honestly had a wonderful time. They knew just about everyone there. Some were surprised she was with him and asked about her fiancé. She said he had gone to California and married someone else. She didn't know where she got the strength to tell these friends without breaking down into tears, but amazingly, she felt calm and assured as she answered their questions.

They continued to see each other at church meetings and to go out every so often. After a lengthy courtship, he asked her to marry him. She knew she loved him, but she was afraid he would leave her like the other man. In reality, she had never gotten over her former fiancé's betrayal. He was her first love and he would always have a piece of her heart. It took her quite a while to commit to a new love, but she finally did.

They had a happy marriage and Evelyn gave birth to a baby daughter. Everything was going along just fine for several years and then her husband died unexpectedly. Again, Evelyn was devastated. Why did he have to die? Why did he leave like this? She couldn't understand, but she had her faith to carry her through.

During the years that she was married, her first fiancé's marriage was falling apart. When it finally ended in divorce, he decided to return to Chicago where he found a good job and a nice apartment. He met up with some of his old friends who told him about Evelyn and about her life after he left. He had come to the conclusion, before he returned to Chicago, that he had made a very big mistake when he married another woman. He should have stuck with Evelyn.

He so wanted to see her, but he didn't want it to seem too obvious. He wasn't sure how mad she still was toward him after what he did to her. So, he arranged to go to a church dance where he knew she would be present. He knew the moment he saw the sparkle in her eye that she had never stopped loving him and he was eager to rekindle their relationship. Evelyn, despite loving him for all these years, was not so sure she wanted to start dating him again. She was still afraid of how much he could hurt her.

Her daughter was sixteen years old now and they had been doing well on their own. Evelyn had a good job and earned enough to provide a nice life for her and her daughter. She had been promoted several times over the years and held a very good position with the company. Her parents as well as her husband's parents had been very supportive through the years. They took care of her daughter while she worked and gave her moral support whenever she needed it. Her parents had been very fond of her husband and were almost as devastated as she was when he died.

At about this same time that her old fiancé entered her life again, Evelyn's mother became ill and had to be hospitalized. Her mother had been her rock for all these years and Evelyn felt as though her world was falling apart. She was so afraid that she would lose her mother. She didn't think she could bear that.

Her instincts were to run to her former fiancé for comfort. She still remembered what it was like to be held in his arms. She could still feel the tickle on her neck as he whispered in her ear. Yes, she wanted him. Even after all these years, he was the most familiar man she knew. Evelyn had not dated in years and was very involved in her church. She joined several of the clubs. Her daughter was also very active in the church. She went to church and prayed about her decision. Should she take a chance with him again? Why didn't his first marriage work out? Had he changed over the years and would he be more faithful to her now?

Then she decided to put thoughts of him aside and focus her prayers for her mother's recovery. As she prayed, she felt a peace that she did not feel when praying about this man. The difference in how she felt was so profound, she knew that she was praying for the wrong thing when she prayed that she could have a solid relationship with him. At last, she had her answer. She called him and told him that she would always love him, but she could never trust him. Then she went to the hospital to be by her mother's side.

In time, her mother got better, but she was not completely well. She told Evelyn that she wished she would marry again so that someone would be there to take care of her. Evelyn just smiled and said, "Yes, mother." Though, as far as I know, Evelyn never remarried.

During the years before I got married, I had watched Evelyn get dumped, marry a different man, have a child, and then lose her husband. We often talked about how she would never get married again. She talked about how painful it was to lose someone you loved. As a result, I decided I would try to guard my heart the best I could until just the right person came along.

Me and my friend Lily

It is necessary to have a tender heart, but not so tender that it leads you to make mistakes. With a great balance of tenderness and intelligence, the interesting things in life are good experiences, not bad. With this recipe, the aim is take a tough heart and make it tender.

BRAISED BEEF HEART
serce wolowe w sosie

Ingredients:

1 beef heart	Water
1 portion of soup greens	Several Peppercorns
1 Bay leaf	2 Grains of allspice
1 clove	

Remove all tubes from the beef heart and wash thoroughly.

Place heart in pot, cover with cold water, bring to boil, then reduce heat, cover, and simmer about 2 1/2 hours. Replace water that evaporates.

Add soup greens, peppercorns, bay leaf, allspice, and clove; continue simmering until heart is tender.

Remove heart and, when cool enough to handle, remove and discard all fat and hard matter. Slice heart and simmer briefly in brown gravy, hot cream sauce, or other hot sauce of choice.

Note: In general, beef heart requires slow long cooking, because it is on the tough side, but can be very tasty if properly prepared. It should be avoided by people with above-normal cholesterol levels.

8

During this time, my favorite girl friend, Lily met a young Jewish man at work and fell head over heels in love with him. She was Italian and came from a devoutly Catholic family. They were so religious that they even had an altar in their living room. Lily's father had died when she was very young and she had been raised by her mother who was always there for her.

Her wedding was a very fancy affair held at a hotel in downtown Chicago. I was unable to attend because I had no way to get there. I now wonder if it seemed as though I didn't support the marriage, but at the time I never imagined her marriage would fall apart so quickly. They parted after only six months of marriage. It was quite controversial at the time for her to have married outside her faith. The divorce was particularly devastating for Lily. She was so sure that theirs was a match made in heaven, but in reality it was a living hell. At the time, I vowed that I would never let myself be hurt this much. I didn't think I could take it.

In the end, Lily did recover, but who could predict that at the time. Eventually, she met another man and after a lengthy courtship, they married. They bought a house and about a year after they were married had their first child. Within a year after that, a second baby was on the way and they were both happy that their union was so blessed.

Lily's mother and sister lived nearby and came over often to help take care of the children and to visit. Her husband never complained that his house was continually full of her relatives. He embraced them as if they were his very own family. She knew that this time she was married to a very good man. A few years later, her mother became very ill and could no longer live alone. Lily asked her husband if he would permit her to have her mother move in. Without hesitation he agreed and her mother moved in.

Lily was very busy with two young children to care for in addition to her mother. Her mother took several medicines throughout the day and had to be kept on schedule. The children were always clean and well dressed for school in the morning and dinner was on the table each evening. Lily's sister came by frequently to help her out and thankfully would often offer to go to the grocery store for her. You would think that this situation would have put pressure on their marriage, but it never did.

After her mom had lived with her for quite awhile, she took a turn for the worse and was hospitalized. She died soon after. Lily's husband was supportive during the entire time and took care of most of the preparations for the funeral. Of course, when I made up my mind not to marry until the right man came along, I hadn't known that Lily would eventually find the perfect mate and have a wonderful future. I just knew how painful her first marriage was when she married the wrong man.

Fish—such a good thing to eat, but the connotations that have come to be associated with fish over the years are many. There are fishy stories, things that smell fishy and of course the exaggerations that come regarding the size of fish caught.

SALMON PATTIES
Ingredients:

1 can salmon, remove liquid
1 dry onion, chopped
2 pieces of white bread (soaked in water)

1 T. of Catsup
Oil

Squeeze water out of bread and add to other ingredients. Mix well.
Divide into 12 sections.
Place one section at a time into lightly oiled pan over a medium heat
Flatten with fork.
As the bottom is browning, turn over to brown the other side. Yum!

Fish can make such a great meal, but if it is left too long in the refrigerator—the odor can be atrocious. Everyone in the house knows you have old fish in the fridge and there is nothing you can do to hide the fact, except to get rid of it. Some incidents in life are just like that. No matter what you do, the smell follows you around for years.

HALIBUT STEAKS
Ingredients:

1 lb. of halibut
Salt
Pepper

Flour
Oil or Lard

Wash halibut—salt and pepper it and coat with flour.
In a frying pan, heat oil or lard.
Place fish in pan and fry until lightly brown.
Turn fish over and again till lightly brown.
Remove from pan and place on paper towels to absorb grease.
Place on platter and serve.

9

As for me, I had met a tall dark haired good looking man at the Aragon Ballroom who owned a tavern. He lived quite a distance from me and when we went to a dance he usually came to my house to pick me up. Both his parents had died and he had inherited their tavern business and their house where he lived alone. I didn't think it was proper to visit in his house with no chaperone. Therefore, I never visited his house or neighborhood.

After we had been dating for a couple of years, he came to me with some very bad news. He said that there was a young girl in his neighborhood who was pregnant. Her boyfriend was unwilling to marry her and her parents were ashamed. He had decided to marry her and take the child as his own. I was very upset at the news, but found that it was honorable of him to make such a sacrifice. He asked me to attend the wedding, but I had no desire to go.

On the day he was to be married, two of his friends came by and picked me up to take me to the wedding. I went even though I was still very hurt by his decision. Of all the men in the world, why did my boyfriend have to be the one to take care of this girl? There was a reception in the church basement after the wedding. He never once asked his bride to dance, because she was very pregnant. He did ask me to dance and I did—one last dance for old times.

It wasn't until years later that I learned that my old boyfriend often had women over to his house during the time we were dating. Everyone in his neighborhood believed that the child his wife carried was his as she had been seen often in his company and entering his house. I suppose in the end I was the lucky one, but at the time it didn't feel as if I was.

My friend Vicky and I
1947

What are the connotations that go along with duck? There is the ugly duckling who became beautiful. There is the childhood game, "duck, duck, goose" where it is the duck who is safe, but the goose who gets tagged. But the best duck is the one who is able to shed water off his back. Not all of us can do this trick, but we wish we could.

DUCK
Ingredients:

1 Large Duck
Salt
Pepper
4 tbsp of Caraway

Remove the giblets from the duck and wash it in and out.
Salt and pepper the inside and outside of the duck. Then sprinkle with caraway.
Place it in a roasting pan and roast at 350 degrees about 1 hour per pound.

While roasting, take a fork and keep on piercing the skin all over the body.
This is to release any fat and needs to be done every 30 minutes.

When duck is getting rather brown, turn down the heat and leave in oven.

After another 10–15 minutes, remove duck from oven and place on platter. It's ready to eat and it should be yum, yum, yum.

Serve it with dumplings or mashed potatoes.

10

I had been on vacation from my job when my girlfriend Vicky and I decided one night to go to the Trianon. We didn't go there often as it was on the south side of Chicago and quite a distance from both our homes. It wouldn't cost us anything as we were both members of the 400 Club. I lived on the north side of Chicago, Vicky lived on the west side so we decided to meet at the ballroom. I took the elevated train by myself.

I arrived at my stop and proceeded to walk a block or so to the Trianon. I became very afraid by the neighborhood, however, I had a date to meet my friend so I had to continue on (this was the first time I did this). As I passed some men standing outside the local pool hall, I could hear them talking among themselves. This made me even more frightened. I made up my mind then that I would never ever go to the Trianon again on the elevated train by myself. I never did! Vicky would either spend the night at my house or if a male friend asked me to go to the Trianon I'd only go if he had an automobile.

Vicky was always happy to stay at my house. We'd take public transportation there. My mother was always elated to see us safely home. By 1944, all of my brothers had gone away to fight in the war so there was a lot of extra space in our house. My mother had become accustomed to having a full house and missed my brothers terribly. When Vicky and I would arrive home, she would be waiting up for us and we often fell to talking about my brothers. While my brother Ed was well over six feet tall, my twin brothers were both 5' 6" and weighed about 135 pounds. Nevertheless, my brother, Lou, became an excellent boxer for his command in the army. He would send news clippings home to us that detailed his bouts. He was a very popular boxer who performed well. For one bout, he won a tiny pair of gold boxing gloves.

Vicky had her own bedroom and bathroom at our house so she slept well. Once we had visited for a bit and had a small snack, we would each go to our own rooms. In the morning she'd shower and get ready for work. Then take off for the streetcar.

The Trianon was even more beautiful than the Aragon; however, the neighborhood was not, so Vicky and I became regulars at the Aragon. One Tuesday evening when the weather was clear but cold, I took the street car to reach the ballroom, however when the dance was over it was after 10 pm so I decided I'd take a cab home. There were several cabs parked outside the ballroom. I decided I'd take the third one in line.

I motioned to the driver. He drove up to me and asked me where I wanted to go. I told him and entered the back seat. I lived about 20 minutes from the dance hall. He drove down one block, stopped the cab, left me in the back seat as he got out of the cab. He didn't explain why he stopped in fact he didn't say a word. The street was dark and not a soul was around. I got a little frightened as I knew that everyone was probably asleep and would not hear me scream if he tried to enter the backseat of the cab. He walked around the cab and then got back into the drivers seat and off we went. I asked why he left the cab. He told me he thought he felt a flat tire. Why didn't he stop at a gas station?

When we reached my house, I paid him and quickly left to enter my house. Everyone was asleep at my house and I didn't turn on any lights when I came in. I watched from the front window to see him leave. He just remained in the cab in front of my house for about 10 minutes then he finally drove off. I was totally afraid and after that, I didn't want to take a taxi home anymore. Many times a male friend of mine would drive to the dance halls and then would drive me home. I felt safer that way.

Family Portrait - 1947
John, Me, Ed, Lydia, Lou
My Mother and Father

When men are talking about cream puffs, what comes to mind immediately? Their cars. Well, as cherished as cars are by some, others of us would rather not be responsible for tons of metal and an engine that roars!

CREAM PUFFS
Ingredients:

1 Cup Water
½ Cup Butter
1 Cup Flour
½ tsp. Salt
4 Eggs
Cool Whip

Heat water and butter to boiling in 3 quart saucepan.
Vigorously stir in flour and salt over low heat until mixture forms a ball.
Remove from heat.
Add eggs, one at a time beating thoroughly after each addition.
Drop by spoonfuls onto baking sheet 2 inches apart.

Bake at 425 degrees for 20 to 30 minutes (until golden brown)

Turn off oven, prick each puff with a fork and return to oven for 20 minutes to dry center.

Cool, cut off tops and fill with Cool Whip.

11

All three of my brothers had been drafted into the service for the war. They served in Europe during World War II. Lou and John were both ambulance drivers. Our house had seemed so empty when they were gone, but with the war over they had returned safe and sound and the house was bustling with family again. Our cousin Stanley had married a girl from Indiana and had moved there so she could be close to her family. Ga was still with us and it seemed like a great reunion.

When the war ended in 1945, my brothers came home. We were so happy to have the family together. So many families we knew had lost a son or brother and we knew how fortunate we were to have had three sons go to war and have all three return. My brother Ed met a lovely woman while in Europe named Lydia. She was from the Ukraine and during my brother's time there they fell in love. They decided to marry and she returned to the United States with him.

Ed decided to go to Northwestern University in Chicago to pursue his degree. My twin brothers, John and Lou, decided to go to college in Texas on the GI Bill. It was sad to see them go, but they were so happy to be living in an area where they could play golf year round.

With the war over and cars being made again, my parents thought it would make things easier if I we had a family car. While neither of them wanted to drive they thought that my brother Ed and I could use the car to go wherever we wanted. They truly thought it would be easier for me to get around and not have to worry about public transportation or cabs anymore. However on Sundays we'd take them where they wanted to go. After my parents had made the deal, Ed and I went to the car dealership and picked up the car. My brother Ed started to drive home. Actually, he drove because I didn't have a driver's license and I really didn't know how to drive.

As we were driving home, Ed stopped the car and asked me to drive. I was reluctant, but I sat behind the wheel and put the car in motion. I drove just a short distance and hit another car. A policeman came by and we told him what happened. After we settled everything, I told my brother it would be best if he drove the rest of the way home and he agreed.

When we arrived home, my parents were waiting on the porch. They were so happy to now have a car in the family. Barely a word was spoken about the damage I caused by the accident and my parents had it repaired quickly. Ed was very good to my parents. He drove them where ever they wanted to go. My mother kept telling me I should try to drive the car, but I always declined.

My brother Ed was very good to me. He knew I loved dancing and so when Saturday came he'd ask me what I'd be doing. I would tell him what was on my schedule then ask him what he was going to do. If he didn't have anything special planned, I would ask him to drive me and a girl friend to the ballroom. There were several ballrooms we'd want to go to, the Aragon, the Trianon, or the Paradise which was located on Pulaski Road. We enjoyed the Paradise on Saturdays because there was always a large crowd there.

We'd dance until about 11:00 pm and then my brother would pick us up. He would usually have a friend with him and we'd go to Russell's Restaurant for barbecue. We all loved their sandwiches and to show my appreciation to my brother Ed, I would buy a sandwich for him.

Ed continued to drive my parents to visit their friends, to go shopping and where ever they wanted to go. There were times when my mom really wanted me to drive her some place and she just couldn't understand why I would not drive. I did try to drive again, but I was so concerned that I would hit another car that I just couldn't concentrate on driving. Fearfully, I would come home after only driving a block or so away.

Ed not only drove my parents around, but he drove me around too. It is a wonder he had any time for himself with all the hours he spent shuttling his family around Chicago. As for me, I had no interest in driving and it would take me over 40 years to change my mind.

Johnny and I out on a date with our friends.

Sometimes two cultures like the same exact thing, but they have different ways of making it. A little more of this and a little less of that and you have something that tastes exactly as you want. If only life was so easily managed!

SULC

2 each Pork Knuckles (Hocks), Fresh
1 each Pork Knuckles (Hocks), Smoked
2 stalks celery, Finely chopped
1 whole onion, finely chopped (medium size)
2 cloves garlic, Crushed
2 tablespoons Relish
2 tablespoons vinegar, Cider
2 teaspoons salt
1 pinch pepper
1 envelope gelatin

Makes 4 Servings

Place all of the above ingredients in pot and cover with water until meat starts to shrink away from the bone. Set up food chopper with the coarse cutter. Remove meat from the bone and put through the cutter. When finished, return to liquid in the pot and continue to cook until the vegetables have practically dissolved (about 1.5 hours). Dissolve 1 envelope of gelatin in 1/2 cup of cold water and add to pot. Continue to cook until mixture resumes boiling. Remove from stove and pour to a depth of 1.5" in a roasting pan. When cooled down and safe to handle, place in lowest shelf in refrigerator and allow to gel and chill. When mixture is cold it should be gelled to about the consistency of Jello. After mixture is well set up, it is ready to eat.

Note: Vinegar may be used as a dressing, as well as salt and pepper.

12

Something wonderful happened to me. I met John Budilovsky. We met at the Trianon Ballroom in June of 1948! He would become my future husband. When we met, we were both members of the 400 Club. He was a member at the Trianon as he lived on the south side of Chicago whereas I belonged to the Aragon as I lived on the north side of Chicago. We would dance with each other at the ballrooms for months until we got to know each other better.

This particular night I saw him standing and watching the other dancers. Our eyes met when a new number began, but I couldn't just go up to him and ask him to dance. As an instructress, I had to go to my station and stand in line and wait for a partner to come and ask me to dance. I always enjoyed meeting new people as we'd laugh and talk as we danced. When I got back in line, it was my turn to be at the front and to dance with the next man who approached. I was so hoping that this man would be the next one to approach the line, but there was someone else who got there first.

When the band went on break, I went upstairs to sit and to have a soft drink. Some dancers I was acquainted with sat with me in a circle of chairs around a table. As we didn't all know each other's names, introductions were made. The chair next to me was empty, but it was introduced as Johnny, who would be there shortly. He had gone to make a phone call before coming upstairs.

I was surprised when the man that sat down next to me was the man I had wanted to dance with earlier in the evening. We started to talk to each other and found that conversation came easy. As it turned out, this was the luckiest day of my life.

Not long after our first meeting, John and I met up again at the Trianon. One of his friends was there along with his date. The four of us went to a nearby ice cream parlor for ice cream and we talked and got to know each other even better. The following week John came to the Aragon where I was an instructress. We danced and talked some more.

As we met each week at the Aragon ballroom, we talked a lot about ourselves. We usually went to the Aragon, but occasionally we frequented the Trianon, or a local church or club dance. We both really loved to dance, but in between dances, we would talk about our life, our work, our dreams and our hopes. It was during one of these dance dates that I told Johnny about my work at Montgomery Ward. He then told me what he did. I was very surprised to learn that he was a mortician. As time went by, he told me more and more about his work. I had always been afraid of the dead but I knew I had to get over that fear if I were to continue seeing Johnny.

Johnny was in his early 30's when we met and had been running the family business for nearly 14 years. His dream had been to go to college and become a doctor, but that did not come to pass. When he was 19, he was enrolled at the University of Chicago and was studying hard to earn a pre-med degree. Suddenly and devastatingly, his father died at a young age interrupting John's life course. His father owned a funeral home and this was the source of family income. Now, he was needed to run the business so he left the University and enrolled in mortician school. While in school he worked along side his mother keeping the business going and he was indeed very busy.

We continued to meet each other at the ballrooms and after quite a few months, he told me that he loved cars and that there was a car show downtown that he planned to go to. Casually, he asked me if I would like to go along. Well, of course I did. I was enthusiastic to be able to spend more time with him as I really enjoyed his company. He agreed to pick me up and take me with him. When we arrived, a friend of his was there with a date and the four us looked at all the cars together. I was glad for this because the guys were very interested in the cars and at least I had someone to talk to. Afterwards, we went out for ice cream and had a very nice time. Johnny took me home after that and said he would see me the next week at the Aragon. He made it clear that this was not a real date, but that we were just going out as friends. I agreed with him whole heartedly although I knew that our relationship would get serious in time.

We did see each other the following week at the ballroom and it seemed like we were much closer than before. When the evening was over, he offered to drive me home. I quickly accepted, and was thrilled at this new development. He was a very good driver and kept up a lively conversation all the way to my house. When we arrived, he turned off the car, which surprised me. I thought he would just drop me off and be on his way, but he continued to talk as we sat in the car. I'm not quite sure how it happened, but all of a sudden he had his arm around my shoulder and he kissed me. It was a wonderful kiss, but as soon as it was over, I had my hand on the door latch and jumped out of the car. I thanked him for the ride and said I would see him the next week. I ran into the house on a cloud. I thought I was so ready for that kiss, but it was so sudden I just didn't know how to react. But, now I knew that he really liked me.

Johnny had told me during our conversations that he liked sulc. This is the Bohemian word for head cheese. Head cheese is not cheese in the traditional manner that is made with milk. It's actually hog parts that are held together in a jelly.

My mother and dad liked kwasena, the Polish word for head cheese. My mother made it often and we loved the taste of it. One particular night, my mother was making kwasena while I was out dancing. Johnny had just started to bring me home each week after dancing and my parents did not really know him yet. When Johnny brought me home you could smell the rich aroma of pork cooking and he asked what my mother was making. As I was telling him, my mother came into the parlor and told us she'd finished making a bowl of sulc and asked Johnny if he would like to taste some.

He went into the kitchen and my mother sliced a piece, put it on a plate and gave it to him. He slowly ate it. My mother was surprised that he ate it so slowly and asked if he liked it or not. He told her it wasn't like sulc because sulc had a great deal of vinegar in it. My mother put a bottle of vinegar on the table and asked Johnny to help himself. He did. He told me that now it tasted more like the head cheese he was familiar with and which he likes. One would think that this would have offended my mother as well as me, but neither seemed to mind and the relationship continued undeterred.

Being a funeral home director meant that Johnny had to be available at a moment's notice to make arrangements when someone passed away. It was a life he had gotten used to and his plans were often interrupted. He always left a phone number with his mother as to where he could be reached and they had an arrangement that someone would always be home to answer the phone.

When Johnny was able to spend the entire evening at the dance, he always insisted on driving me home. This was very nice of him because if we were at the Trianon, he would have to drive an hour to get me home and then another hour to get his house. If we were at the Aragon, it would only take twenty minutes to take me home, but then he still had an hour ride to his house. I was always very grateful that he took the time to drive me to my house.

**Johnny and Me
Love is blooming!**

If only life was as foolproof as cooking. I was lucky in love when I found my future husband…and that's no fooling!

FOOL PROOF ROAST BEEF TENDERLOIN
Ingredients:

Beef Tenderloin (room temperature)
Melted Butter
Salt and Pepper

Preheat oven to 450 degrees.
Brush meat with melted butter then season with salt and pepper
Place in shallow pan.
Bake for 15 minutes in 450 degree oven.
Reduce heat to 350 degrees and bake an additional 15 minutes.
Remove from oven, cover with aluminum foil and let stand for
10 to 15 minutes before slicing.

HORSE RADISH
1 Horse Radish (grated)
1 Small Beet (sliced)
Vinegar
Sugar

In a small sauce pan, bring enough vinegar to cover sliced beet to a boil.
When boiling add beet slices and remove from heat.
Let sit until vinegar is cold.
Grate radish into bowl.
Pour vinegar over radish and add about ½ tsp. of sugar. Stir.
Pour into bottle.

13

John had become very fond of me and in the fall asked me out for our first real date. The date was set for October 31, 1948 and was a Halloween party being thrown by a club he belonged to. I dressed up as a gypsy for the party. When Johnny came to pick me up, he had on a clown suit, however, when I saw his face he didn't have any make up on. I asked him to sit down and he let me make up his face so he would look more like a clown. He did and I really put a lot of make-up on his face. Using lipstick, I made big red circles on his cheeks and the tip of his nose and now he truly looked like a clown.

We drove to the party which was held in the back room of a tavern near his house. When we arrived one of Johnny's buddies met us at the car and told him that he needed to call home immediately. Well, he knew what that meant. Someone had died and he needed to attend to the preparations. He told me he'd have to leave but that he would be back to take me home.

It never occurred to me to be real disappointed that on our first date he left me. I stayed at the party and danced with several of his friends. Then, as I was dressed as a gypsy, I decided to start telling fortunes. I was careful to keep things light and only tell good things. This was a big hit and the night passed quickly.

When Johnny arrived home, his mother told him that a neighbor had died and he needed to go to the deceased's house and remove the body. She added that he could not possibly go looking like he did. He went to the bathroom and tried to remove all the make-up I had put on his face, but try as he did, it wouldn't come off. He asked his mother to help and she told him to put Vaseline on his face and try washing it off again. That helped, but it still didn't remove all the make-up. Finally, he gave up, hoping that these friends of his would understand and he went to take care of the body.

He called his service to remove the body from the house and deliver it to his morgue. He sat down with the family and asked as to what papers they wanted the death notice placed and asked for some personal information regarding the deceased person. Once he was finished with all the preliminary preparations he told his mother that he was going to return to the party. It was almost midnight, but she encouraged him to go back to the party. She would take care of whatever else needed to be done that night and the rest he could take care of in the morning. His mother, Josephine, had often assisted her deceased husband in the business and knew what had to be done.

Johnny returned to the party just as it was ending and took me home. I had a great time, but I wished we could have spent more time together on our first date.

For our second date, he asked me to go with him to the Undertakers Ball. This was a formal affair that was attended by all the Bohemian undertakers in the area. Johnny was the president of the Bohemian Undertakers at that time and as such was required to lead a procession into the banquet room where the dinner would be served. As his date, he escorted me down the center aisle to the head table. We had dinner, danced and had a very good time. John introduced me to many of his fellow undertaker friends. When the evening was over he drove me home and kissed me goodnight and told me he would see me on Tuesday at the Aragon. I was very happy that I would be able to see him again.

Of course, when I began dating Johnny I never knew if we'd be able to do whatever we had planned on doing because there were many, many times when we'd planned on going to a club dance and the phone rang and Johnny needed to immediately change all plans because he had work to do. I knew what he did for a living. I began to accept last minute changes.

He was glad that it didn't bother me to change plans at the last minute. I realized this was his work and no one knows when a death will occur. Therefore his work needed to be taken care of first, if we still had time, we could go out and do whatever we were able to do. He wanted to spend time with me, but because of his business it didn't always work out that way.

When Johnny would ask me out for a date, he'd often bring me a corsage. Of course his thoughtfulness was delightful and it was the best way to accent my favorite dress. He was always thinking about me.

There was something about Johnny that caught my eye and as I got to know him better, I began to realize that I loved him and everything about him. I realized he was a very good and kind person. He was exactly the kind of person I'd like to know more.

This went on for several months. He'd drive to the Aragon, we'd dance together. We would then have ice cream during intermission and then he would drive me home. We were getting to know each other better and getting to like each other more.

One evening, Johnny came to my house and asked if I wanted to go to Riverview Park. It was a well known amusement park near my neighborhood. I told him I'd like to go as I hadn't been there for many years—since I was a young girl. I put on a pair of slacks and off we went in his car. It was a Thursday night so all the rides and admission where just 5 cents. We walked in and the first ride was a fast moving roller coaster. I was a little afraid to go on the roller coaster and so we decided to walk further down the midway. After a short distance, there was a booth that held various attractions. I decided I'd sit on a bench outdoors and watch the performers as they came out to show themselves and promote the shows inside. After seeing who was inside I didn't care to see the show.

We continued on and saw the "Shoots" not far ahead. This was a ride that we both liked. We purchased our tickets and boarded a small boat that was taken by elevator to the top of a huge slide. We sat at the top for a short while as we were given instructions on how we should act and what was in store for us. Within a short time, we heard a horn which meant we'd be leaving the top of the slide and would be going down into a pool of water. This was exciting. Many in the boat began to scream while others laughed loudly. Down we went and soon we hit the water. Those sitting in the front seat got wet. We had watched this ride and so we decided we'd sit in the middle of the boat so as not to get wet. This was a thrilling ride and we went on it several times. Riverview Park no longer exists except in our memories. Nowadays amusement parks are like Six Flags and the Disney Theme Parks which are much newer and modern.

I don't believe I ever complained to Johnny because of where he wanted to go even though there were times when I wasn't in the mood to go wherever it was that he wanted to go. Perhaps it was a dance or a play. I was never too eager to go to a Bohemian play because I didn't always understand everything. However, before we went Johnny would explain everything to me, so that in the end I would really enjoy the play.

I realized I was honestly falling in love with this man who couldn't always keep a date with me. If it were any other man, I would have told him, "So long." I felt he was beginning to care a lot for me too. I never complained to him that he left me on my own here or there.

Happy Birthday, Lee

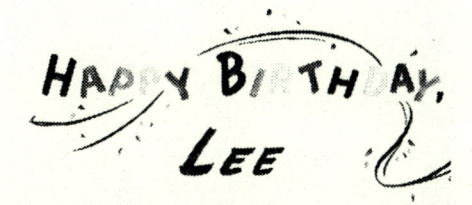

A birthday card from Johnny!

Some foods are known as comfort foods. We eat them when we feel lost or down. We eat them when we fill sick or anxious. Chicken Dumpling Soup is one of these elixirs. Just the smell of it cooking can bring a smile to anyone's face. It has always been my daughter Jane's favorite dish.

CHICKEN DUMPLING SOUP
Ingredients:

1 Chicken
Water
1 Carrot
1 Onion
2 Stalks of Celery
Spices of your choice

Cut up chicken into small pieces. Place in pot and cover with water.
Bring to a boil over a medium flame.
Remove any white foam from top.
Add carrot peeled and cut into small pieces, onion pealed and chopped into pieces, and celery cut into ¼ inch pieces.
Add spices to taste
Bring back to a boil. Boil about 30 minutes.
Chicken pieces can be removed and eaten separately or the chicken can be removed from the bone, cut up into smaller pieces and returned to liquid.

DUMPLINGS
Ingredients:

1 Cup Flour
1 or 2 T. of Fat
1 Egg

Mix together all ingredients to form a batter.
Take a tablespoon of the mixture and place into boiling soup.
Keep putting tablespoons of mixture into soup until all batter is gone.
The batter will cook into dumplings.
Boil soup with dumplings for about additional 30 minutes.

14

Johnny belonged to many clubs and just about every club held a dance once a year. Johnny felt he needed to be present at all the dances and he would invite me to come along. I always accepted. When we went to a dance, I'd meet many of his friends. We danced and really enjoyed ourselves.

One club, Athlon Philoi continued during World War II even though most of the male members were overseas in the service. Johnny was exempt from the service because of his work in the funeral home. So he kept the girls in the club busy with a variety of projects many of them for the war effort. The girls often met to write letters to their boyfriends. Johnny had many friends overseas and he would write letters too. They would meet once a month and read the letters that the club members had received from overseas. It was a sad time and a happy time for all in the club.

Finally, the war was over and the fellows returned. The meetings continued and the club got larger. By the time I started going with Johnny to club events, several of the couples had married and had children. The children always came with their parents to the club meetings.

Athlon Philoi, is now over 50 years old and we still get together but not as regularly as we did before. There are many of our members who have gone home to heaven and no doubt they are watching us from above.

Cards and letters were always an important way for Johnny to communicate and he showered me with cards, poems and letters. One of his good friends was an artist and Johnny would ask him to make special cards for me. I was always delighted to see what they had come up with together. For my birthday one year I received a very personalized card that had a caricature of him. I loved the brightly colored card and have kept it to this day, over 50 years later.

Another time, I had gone on a "Happiness Tour" for vacation. It was a two week tour that started in Chicago and headed west with stops along the way. Our final destination was California before we started back. Depending on where we were going, we either rode in a bus or took a train. It was a very exciting trip and I was able to see so much of the United States.

When we reached our destination, you can imagine my surprise when there was a card waiting for me from Johnny. Again, he had his friend, George Bures, design the card and when I received it, I knew how much he missed me. Even though I was having a terrific time, after getting the card, I was anxious to get home.

— AND HOW'S MY FAVORITE BLONDE?

Thought you might enjoy having me show you the tour personally —

so here I am!

The card I received from Johnny when I was on my "Happiness Tour"

Lou and John—wonderful brothers
and great golfers.

We all come to a point in our life when we find that it is what's on the inside that counts. It is not necessarily the heart that beats that keeps us alive, but the spirit that inhabits the heart. When we find the person whose heart beats in time with our own, then a match is made that can never be broken.

CHOCOLATE-FILLED SNOWBALLS
Ingredients:

1 Cup Margarine
½ Cup Sugar
1 tsp. Vanilla
2 Cups Flour
1 Cup Walnuts (finely chopped)
1–5 ½ oz. package of Chocolate Kisses
Confectioner' Sugar

Beat sugar, margarine and vanilla until light and fluffy.
Add flour and nuts—blend well. Chill
Remove foil from kisses. Shape dough around each kiss using about 1 tbsp. of dough.
Be sure to cover kisses completely.

Bake at 375 degrees on an un-greased cookie sheet for 12 minutes.
Cool slightly.
While still warm, roll in confectioner's sugar.

Makes 40 cookies

15

My brother Ed and his wife Lydia were living at home with my parents. Ed wanted to get a Masters Degree and was attending Northwestern University. John and Lou attended Hardin-Simmons University in West Texas.

Both Lou and John were becoming well known for their golfing successes in the Southwest. They had won several tournaments in college and were very pleased when they took first and second place titles. Lou had met a very nice gal, Betty, in Texas and we knew that he was thinking about marriage himself. Betty was a nurse and was very compassionate. Her tenderness touched my brother and he fell head over heels in love with her. As she was from the Southwest, we expected that he would stay in that area and not return to Chicago. And that is what happened. He found that he loved the desert atmosphere of Arizona and eventually settled there in a house located on a bluff overlooking a picturesque panorama.

John returned home for awhile, but his heart was set on traveling and seeing the world. His plan was to be a school teacher so he would have his summers free to explore and do the things he wanted. This he did until he met a woman named Margie and they settled down in California. Margie was also a school teacher and this enabled them both to spend their summers in just the manner they wanted.

When Ed graduated from Northwestern, he started working for Western Electric, where he had a very good job. Now that they were financially on their feet Ed and Lydia really wanted a house of their own. They had been looking at different villages in the suburbs of Chicago and finally found a nice house in the town of Westchester. This was about an hour ride away from my parent's house on the north side of Chicago.

They had found a wonderful ranch house located in an area that had all new houses with young couples just starting their families. This was perfect for them as they were starting their family and their neighbors were all around their age. Ed joined the many men of his community who commuted to work each day, leaving their wives behind to raise the family and keep the house. They purchased a beautiful house in a beautiful neighborhood.

They were very happy, in fact, we were all happy for them. They slowly bought furniture for their new house and Lydia did a fine job decorating. Ed still came into the city and drove my mother shopping once a week and she was very thankful for that.

Ed and his wife Lydia enjoyed their suburban life. They had a son and a daughter that they absolutely loved. They were darling children and at times I longed to have a family of my own when seeing how beautiful Ed's family was.

Ed bought a small out door grill and on weekends he'd invite several of the neighbors over to his house for a barbecue. As all the couples were struggling to make ends meet, it was more of a potluck, with Ed providing the meat and the neighbors bringing side dishes for everyone to enjoy. Everyone looked forward to these events because they got to know each other better. Johnny and I would drive out to their house on weekends too. We were introduced to the neighbors and we all got along very well.

Around this time, Ga started to look tired and worn out. Nevertheless, he went to work at Carson's every day and did his job. One day while he was at work, he felt unusually bad and decided to go to the nurse's station and see if she could do something to make him feel better.

When he arrived at the office, the nurse could see that he was not doing well and helped him to the sick bed where he laid down. She did not know that he was in the midst of a heart attack and wouldn't have been able to aid him much if she did. The attack was massive and he died He had lived with our family for over twenty-five years, had never married, and we were the only family he had.

When my parents told me of his death, I was distraught. He was an uncle to me and I had always been fond of him. I didn't want just anyone to handle his funeral so with my parents' agreement, I called Johnny because I knew he would take care of everything with respect and great detail.

By this time I knew that Johnny and I would marry and that I would be laid to rest along side him at the Bohemian National Cemetery where his family had their plot. As my parents were the first generation of their family to live in the United States, they had no family plot here. I also knew that they would not want Ga to be alone. So, we bought a nice plot at the Bohemian National Cemetery that would accommodate Ga, my mother and father. Johnny did a wonderful job with the funeral. My three brothers and my cousin Stanley were among the six pall bearers.

My twin brothers, Lou and John both decided to major in education in college and went on to become teachers and principals. Both were becoming known as seasoned golfers and gave lessons to celebrities who sought them out. It was amazing how equal their talent was in this area. Their forte was long hitting and they often shut out competitors from winning any holes in a tournament.

After a brief respite of having the house full just like it was before the war, it was now feeling rather empty. There was my mom, dad, my brother John and I in this huge house and now I was wondering who would be the next to leave.

Johnny and me on our wedding day with my mother and father.

Johnny and me getting ready to leave on our honeymoon.

In life, there are so many experiences to choose from that certainly there will be something that suits you just right. Some experiences are so sweet that you remember them forever...just like these brownies and kolackies.

BEST EVER BROWNIES
Ingredients:

1 cup of butter or margarine
1 ¾ cups of sugar
1 cup of flour
1 cup of chopped nuts

4 squares of chocolate
4 eggs
2 tsp of vanilla

In a saucepan, melt butter and chocolate. Cool slightly.
Add sugar, eggs (one at a time), flour, and vanilla.
Beat well. Fold in nuts
Pour into greased 9" X 13" pan and spread evenly
Bake at 350 degrees for 25 to 30 minutes.

CREAM CHEESE KOLACKY
Ingredients:

1 cup of butter or margarine
2 cups of flour
1 8oz. pkg of cream cheese
Apricot Jam

Cream together—cream cheese and butter.
Add flour and mix thoroughly.
Roll out thin and cut out circles using a small glass.
Place ½ tsp. of apricot jam in the center of each circle.
Place on cookie sheet and bake at 374 degrees until light brown.

16

The months that I had known Johnny seemed to fly by and soon it was February 14, 1950—Valentines Day. He brought a box of chocolates to my house, kissed me and wished me a "Happy Valentine's Day." I was so very happy to receive the chocolates which meant he was thinking of me on this special day. What really surprised me was that he also wrote a poem. I was very happy to be cared for enough that someone would write me a poem. The poem was as follows:

> *I've had other loves,*
> *Yes I had.*
> *To deny it would not*
> *Be for an honest lad.*
> *When on memories canvas*
> *I paint my loves,*
> *Beauties galore amongst*
> *Fluttering doves.*
> *There's one who will*
> *Outshine the rest*
> *That is you darling,*
> *The best.*

I knew I had very strong feelings for him, but this was the first indication that he had really strong feelings for me too. Although we were both secure in our feelings for each other, nothing changed in our relationship at first. We continued to meet every Tuesday night at the Aragon to dance and occasionally went out on a date.

Spring melted into summer and our relationship continued to get stronger. It was a beautiful Saturday night in August and Johnny and I had planned on going out together. It wasn't decided where we'd go or what we'd do that night except that we would be together. It was 7:00 PM and the door bell rang. I answered and Johnny was all dressed up. I was so happy to see him again. As we prepared to leave he told me it would be best if I brought a sweater with me as it was getting cooler out doors. I asked where we were going and he coyly responded, "You'll see when we get there."

We got into his car and drove out to the University of Chicago where he had attended school. He then led me to a small chapel where he told me that he would come whenever he had a problem of some sort and he would pray. We both sat quietly in a pew. John asked to be excused for a moment as he had something he needed to get from his car. I told him I would wait here until he returned.

He was gone for about a half an hour and I began to worry. I started to think, 'I hope he doesn't forget I'm here because I don't know how to get back to my house.' Then I saw him at a distance and I was relieved that he was on his way back to where I was. I stood to greet him and he hugged and kissed me then told me he was sorry he was gone so long. When he had gotten back to the street, it appeared he couldn't find his car. Then he told me that he knew he loved me and hoped that I loved him too.

He took a small package from his jacket and started to open it. He then handed it to me so I could finish opening it. Inside the paper was a small box with a ring inside. I looked at it. It was a beautiful diamond ring. He asked me to try it, but with my eyes so filled with tears of joy, he had to help me put it on my finger. This was the beginning of a great romance. He asked me to marry him and I accepted. I was in heaven!! I loved Johnny and now Johnny told me he loved me too.

We began to talk about wedding plans. He asked me where I would like to be married and where I would like to have the reception afterwards. I told him that I didn't want a big wedding party. "Let's just have a small dinner at my mother's house. She'll be happy to prepare it for us. We'll invite our family and our friends that we will ask to be witnesses to the marriage." Then he told me that he had a very good friend who could officiate at the wedding and asked if that would be okay with me. I said yes and we continued to make our plans.

We thought it would be best to marry in the fall. We then picked the date of October 21st. This date later became "Sweetest Day". It sure was the "sweetest day" for Johnny and me!

The next Tuesday night, when we went to the dance as we did every Tuesday night, I wore my ring and showed if off. Johnny and I were congratulated by all of our friends there. Johnny and I were both very happy having been promised to each other.

We were married on October 21st, 1950, by a local minister, Dr. Charles August Chval, a good friend of Johnny's from the Lawndale neighborhood. The ceremony took place in his living room. His daughter Olga and her husband belonged to the same neighborhood club that Johnny and I did called the Athlon Philoi.

Johnny had been married before and did not want a big ceremony again, so we had a small wedding with only family and a few friends present in the minister's house. I wore a beige suit that was beautifully tailored by my mother. It seemed more appropriate for a wedding in a house and it looked stunning with the corsage that Johnny brought me when he came to pick me up at my mother's house.

Johnny had asked a friend of his to take pictures during the ceremony and after. He did a wonderful job and we have many memorable photos of the occasion. Then he asked us to stop by his studio on our way to my mother's house so he could take a portrait of us together. We agreed to do that.

We were surprised when we left the minister's house, to see a group of our friends waiting for us on the sidewalk. They showered us with rice and yelled their congratulations. We thanked them and promised to get together after we got back from our honeymoon.

After having our picture taken John and I drove to my parent's house, where my mother was preparing our first meal as husband and wife. His mother, Josephine, rode in the car with us after the ceremony so she could attend the dinner. My mother made a traditional Polish meal with roast pork, potatoes and salad. The witnesses of our ceremony were also invited. They were George and Genevieve Kralik. George was a neighbor of Johnny's and a good friend. They were married a month before us. My brother, John Turlo, also came to our wedding.

Our wedding was small and intimate with only a few guests. My brother John was living with my parents at the time and he drove them to our wedding. My brother Ed was having health problems so he was unable to attend. My other brother Lou was living in Texas at the time and was also unable to attend. I wished they all could have come on this special day.

I also missed my friend, Vicky, who had spent so many nights at my parent's house after we went out dancing. Vicky and I had worked together at Montgomery Ward and even though she was older than I was, we had a great deal of fun together. Vicky had diabetes and had to be very careful with her health. One night when she was playing cards at her brother's house she collapsed. She was taken to the hospital in a diabetic coma where she died very suddenly. I have no doubt that she was watching from heaven and remembering all the good times we had together.

Vicky and I were very much alike. We both loved to dance and we enjoyed each other's company. Sometimes we'd just eat at a nearby restaurant and go to wherever we wanted to go to dance. When Vicky died, I missed her very much.

After the dinner was over, we thanked everyone for sharing this special day with us. We then drove Johnny's mother home and headed for the Edgewater Beach Hotel where we planned to start our honeymoon.

Our honeymoon was a time of happiness and freedom.

We had so much fun exploring the south and being like kids without responsibility

Our honeymoon at the Paradise Motel in New Orleans

In Cuba...at El Moro.

When we start out, where we end up can be a mystery. How can we know what life holds in store for us? Enjoy the ride and go where the wind blows!

KUBA
Ingredients:

2 Cups mushrooms
1 cup barley
1/2 cup duck fat or butter
1/4 teaspoon pepper 1 teaspoon salt
2 cloves garlic
1/4 teaspoon dried Spanish onion

Cook barley according to package instructions.
In a separate pan, cook fresh mushrooms, drain, and reserve liquid
(Do not cook canned mushrooms just add to other ingredients along with liquid from can)
Add and mix other ingredients.

Put into 9 x 13-inch pan and use 1 1/2 cups of the mushroom juice to pour over the mixture in pan.

Bake slowly 30 minutes at 350 degrees and serve hot.

17

We spent our first night together at the Edgewater Beach Hotel in Chicago. It was a beautiful warm night and before we went to bed we looked out of our window onto the dance floor and watched the guests as they danced. It was beautiful and the music was soft and soothing. We watched for awhile to see if we knew anyone there that night. For a short time we thought we'd go down and dance, however after talking and thinking about it, we decided we would just watch from the window.

The following morning we got up and went downstairs for breakfast. At that time, meals were served at large tables in the dining room. We sat at a table for twelve as we had our first breakfast as husband and wife. We were in a hurry to get on the road and start our honeymoon. I didn't know exactly where we would be going, but I had packed clothes for warm weather.

Johnny had just bought a brand new 1950 black Pontiac with Van Auken Guards on the bumper. Since car manufacturing had stopped during the war, it seemed like such a luxury to have a new one. It was a beautiful car! Its top speed was around 90mph, but Johnny usually kept the speed under 60mph. It got 15 miles to the gallon and at that time gas was around 20 cents per gallon. We put our suitcases in the trunk after checking out of the hotel and headed down the road.

Johnny then surprised me with a wonderful honeymoon. First, he drove us to New Orleans, then along the gulf coast to Florida. The ride along the coast was magical. We also flew to Cuba, which was very exciting.

When we got to Florida, we were looking for a motel to stay at. We came to one we rather liked and were about to check for room availability when a cleaning woman nodded at me as if she knew me. I stopped thinking perhaps she was someone I knew. I talked to her for just a short while and then she asked me if I was Maureen O'Hara. Maureen O'Hara was a beautiful movie star and I was astonished to think she thought I looked like her. I walked up to my husband and told him and he just laughed. I felt foolish. I thought maybe there was something about me that made her think I was Maureen. My husband told me I was pretty, but didn't look like her. I felt a little hurt for a while, but then I was myself again. My husband loved me for myself and not because I looked like someone else.

While in Florida, we visited one of Johnny's former neighbors from Chicago. The family had sold the restaurant they owned which was located next door to Johnny's funeral home. They bought property in Florida where they built another restaurant. They seemed to be very happy with Florida and the location of their new restaurant.

Helen, who was the daughter of this family, had been communicating with Johnny by mail. Therefore, he wanted to see her, her family and the restaurant. I think she had a crush on Johnny. We drove to the restaurant when we got to Florida. Helen happened to be working that day. Johnny recognized her immediately and she recognized him too. She was very happy to see Johnny.

Introductions were made and he told her we were thinking about possibly going to Cuba and asked if she had been there. She told us she was there and that since we were so close we should see it too. She told us where we should stay and what to expect. We listened and then Johnny and I began talking among ourselves. What should we do?

Helen said she would drive us to the airport where we could buy tickets and get on the next plane. And, as we drove, I packed our suitcases while sitting in the back seat.

Should we go or shouldn't we? I kept asking myself as Johnny also asked himself. Well, we were now at the airport and the next plane would be ready in about a half an hour. This would be my first time in an airplane. We decided to go. We were very pleased that there were still tickets available when we got to the airport. If we didn't go, we both knew we would be sorry.

After a short wait, there was an announcement made for all going to Cuba to step up and enter the plane. I was a little frightened as I had never flown in an airplane before. Johnny had flown before and was very calm. We walked up together and sat down together. Within a short time the stewardess came by and asked if we wanted a drink. I didn't drink liquor and so I didn't accept any however, my husband did accept a drink.

It was a short ride and now we were in Cuba. We walked off the plane together and Johnny carried our one piece of luggage. After taking a cab into Havana, we found the hotel where we intended to spend the night.

Johnny knew many people. I thought this would be the one place where Johnny wouldn't know anyone. Wrong. We were standing at one of the two registers of our hotel, which was the Parkview Hotel in Havana off the Del Prado. I happened to hear the gentleman at the other register saying he was from Chicago, so I told John. The gentleman heard me and glanced over and immediately called, "Johnny?"

He happened to be someone of American Cuban descent who Johnny knew. He was a ticket man at the Medinah Ballroom in Chicago on Sundays. His name was Jindriguez. He happened to be in Cuba on business. He was a South American rep for Dr. Scholl's Foot Products and he was making his semi-annual business trip there. That same day, he took us all around Cuba on a bus. He showed us many clubs and restaurants and even took us to a "locals" Cuban restaurant where we dined on delicious food. We were only there for a couple of days, but John's friend Jindriguez sure did help to make our stay in Cuba very enjoyable.

My mother-in-law Josephine

On those hot summer evenings before air-conditioning, there was nothing better than a nice cold soup to make you feel refreshed again. This was one of the favorites.

COLD BEET SOUP (Chlodnik)
Ingredients:

Large bunch of beet tops (stems and leaves)
1 or 2 beet roots
2 or 3 salted pickled gherkins—preferably Polish
Some of the pickle juice
Fresh cucumber, dill, onion, chives
Creme fraîche, sour cream or yogurt or a mixture of these
Concentrated veal stock
Cold fried veal chops or pork tenderloin, cut into small cubes (good, but optional)
Lemon

The evening before you make the soup, grate a beet finely and leave it overnight in a bowl with a little water added.

The next day, chop the beet tops, put them in a pot and pour 2 ½ cups of boiling water over them. Put a fire under the pot and allow them to come to a boil once more. Take off the stove. Dice the cucumber and the pickles. Large or small cubes are a matter of preference. Squeeze the juice from the grated beet and pour juice in a pot. Set grated beet aside.

Add pickle juice, creme fraîche and/or yogurt to pot. Add boiled beet, cucumber and pickles, and give it a stir. Add some of that veal stock, just enough to make a change in the taste. Add the cold meat if you wish. Season with freshly chopped dill, chives and very finely chopped or grated onion. Now, if you like the soup to have a bit more color, add some of the leftover grated beet, or better still, some freshly grated. Finally, salt, pepper and maybe a squeeze of a lemon wedge will bring it to perfection. Chill for a few hours before serving.

A basket of good rye and/or crusty bread on the table is a must!

Serves 4 as a main dish.

18

Upon our return from our honeymoon, I moved into the family home with Johnny and his mother, Josephine, located above the funeral home. We had the large bedroom and Johnny's mother took the smaller bedroom next to ours. The phone was located in the kitchen so that either Johnny or his mother could answer it quickly. No one else was allowed to answer the phone. However, as time went on, I was given permission to answer it. Partly because I took the initiative to learn Bohemian which is what most of Johnny's customers spoke.

One night shortly after we returned from our honeymoon, Johnny and I had attended a neighborhood dance and when we returned home, Johnny drove into the garage and turned off the motor. I walked straight ahead to the door that opened into the morgue. I looked inside and there was a body lying on the embalming table. The table was empty when we left home so I wondered who this was. Johnny walked into the office and noticed papers on the desk that no doubt were delivered with this body. It happened to be a neighbor man who lived on the same block the funeral home was on. Johnny looked at the death certificate and noticed it was a heart attack. He thought he'd contact the doctor the following day since it was so late. It was necessary that a doctor sign the death certificate before any work could be done on the body.

The following day the certificate was signed and the body was ready to be shown. The family came to the office and told Johnny what newspapers they wanted the death notice in. Johnny asked them several questions and prepared the death notice. He read it to them and they agreed as to how it was to be written. They wanted it in the English papers and the Bohemian papers (hence he was a Bohemian and had many Bohemian friends). He was waked for 2 nights and the burial followed. Oh I was learning the funeral business.

Before I was married, I was employed and received a paycheck every week. I had money to buy whatever I wanted. Sometimes I would get a new dress or new shoes. Soon after I was married, I left my job and now had no money of my own. This was a big change for me as I started working when I was 16 and I was now 28 years old. Of course most of the money went to help my parents with their household expenses, but there was always enough left for me too.

My mother was a thrifty person. My father never received a big paycheck but with his small paycheck my mother made it go far. She checked the paper for sales at the local food stores and markets. She was always able to buy food when it was on sale. She also bought dress material when it was on sale. She never bought anything just for the sake of buying it. If she didn't need something, she didn't buy it.

During the depression, my father, brothers and I often went to a church that was a short distance from our house to get free loaves of bread. My mother was so grateful for the gift. There were times when money was so tight that my mother would make 5 sandwiches out of one hot dog using the free bread.

Any money she had left over from shopping she would take to the bank and put it towards the house we lived in or bought needed furniture, rugs or other items for the house. Despite the fact that we never had much money, my mother always kept her children well dressed. Many times when she saw yard goods on a huge sale, she would think of what she could make out of it and if it was something that we needed. Once she answered those questions she would either buy the fabric or forget it.

She did laundry every week and had a vegetable garden which also needed her attention. My father raised rabbits in a part of our garage. My brothers and I considered them our pets. One time my brothers checked the rabbit area and noticed there was one missing. The following Sunday, my mother served roasted rabbit. It was very tasty; however, my brothers made the connection to the missing rabbit and refused to eat it. My twin brothers were very smart and very athletic. It was hard to put one over on them. After that my mother never served rabbit again. Instead, my father sold the rabbits to others who enjoyed their meat.

My new life with Johnny and his mother living over a funeral home was quite a change for me. Most of my friends had their own homes or apartments after they got married and were able to pick out furniture and decorate as they saw fit. I moved into a ready made household that had its own set of rules and habits and was fully furnished.

Johnny's mother liked soup and in fact, she made very good soup. It was their custom to have soup every day for lunch. I disliked soup and wished for anything but soup for lunch. But, to get along, I drank soup everyday at lunchtime.

Josephine, Johnny's mother, had always done the grocery shopping and she bought what she and Johnny liked to eat. When Johnny noticed that I did not find the food as appetizing they did, he started putting a small amount of money in an old purse of his mother's that was hanging in our closet. I could use the money to do shopping of my own and buy things to make that I liked. This solved the problem and on the nights when I would cook, they would be treated to something new and special.

On Sundays, we rarely cooked. It always seemed like Sundays were the busiest day of the week and there was never time to make a decent meal. There happened to be a restaurant next door that served good food. One of us would gather up some pots and head over to the restaurant where they would fill them up with wholesome stews, meats, soups and vegetables. It was not uncommon back then to see cars pulling up to the curb in front of the restaurant all day on Sunday with women emerging with their pots to be filled for a Sunday feast.

Laundry was sent out once a week to be done. As Johnny's mother also worked in the funeral home, it was decided that some household duties had to be sent out. We did, however settle into a routine where whoever had the time did dishes and cleaned house. Usually this was Josephine, John's mother, but I helped whenever I could.

Johnny was an only child and his mother needed him. He loved her. I knew that the three of us would always be together so I tried to make the best of the situation. This was not always easy as Josephine was very set in her ways. But, as the years went by I learned as to what a Godsend it was to have her as a mother-in-law. She truly became a blessing once we had our children.

Johnny had an uncle that lived a few blocks from our house. He helped Johnny at times and I got to know him well. He was a kind man and a good listener. Often times when I felt frustrated or didn't know how to cope with a problem, I would walk over to his house where we would sit on the front porch and he would let me talk. He rarely gave advice as he sensed that I could work things out on my own but just needed a confidant.

Uncle Will became a close friend and someone I could depend on. If a call came in when Johnny and his mother were gone, I would immediately call Uncle Will and he would help me take care of things until I could get in touch with Johnny. He was very patient and stayed with me until everything that needed to be done was done.

Of course, as time went by, I learned more and more about the business and there came a time when I could handle things on my own. While I didn't rely on him for funeral assistance as much, I still enjoyed our time together on the porch solving the mysteries of life. How fortunate I was to have this special man in my life!

Needless to say, no one was more special than my husband. He was my chauffer for most of our married life. He was always happy to drive me where ever I wanted to go. Of course, I hated to ask him to take me everywhere so I would take public transportation whenever possible.

Once there was a bridal shower for the fiancée of a close friend of Johnny's and I was invited to the party. All the seats had been pre-assigned at the banquet hall and I was led to a seat and sat down. I knew several of the women sitting near me and we immediately began to chat, catching up on family news.

After a short time, another young lady was led to the seat across the table from me. We introduced ourselves to each other and began talking. I realized then that this woman was my husband's first wife. I began to feel uncomfortable and I think she felt the same. Why would the person who planned the seating do this? We continued to talk to each other as what else could we do.

Before long, the gifts were all opened and it was time for us to have some coffee and then leave. As I didn't know how to drive, Johnny had dropped me off at the restaurant and I had set a time for him to pick me up. Now I wished I had set the time much earlier. Checking my watch every few seconds, I wished for the hands of time to move more swiftly. Finally, it was close enough to the appointed pick up time that I was able to excuse myself and go outside to wait.

No one can imagine how happy I was to see his car come around the corner and stop at the curb to pick me up. Luckily, his ex-wife hadn't had the same arrangement where she would have had to come outside at the same time and wait for a ride.

Johnny and I decided not to attend the wedding. It would be too uncomfortable for us to be there together along with his ex-wife. We sent our best wishes and a present for the bride and groom.

An incident comes to mind of a time I was taking the street car to my mother's house after we were married. This one beautiful afternoon as I rode the street car I was sitting by an open window. I saw a group of boys standing at the corner and they had buckets in their hands. As the street car drove closer to them, they were ready to do what they intended to do. That was to empty the buckets of water into the open windows of the street car. Thank goodness there was someone other than myself sitting next to the window at the time. The water was thrown in and we all got wet. The motorman stopped the car to get these young boys, however, they were fast and quickly were gone, buckets and all. When I got off the street car, I was dripping wet. I arrived home and I told my husband what had happened. He wanted to call the police. I told him, "Don't bother, they're gone by now and no doubt have another place to go to do this."

I'm sorry now that I stopped my husband from notifying the police. However, I was afraid that if they found out who reported them, they'd do more harm. The next time I rode the street car, which was a long time later, and came to that intersection, I looked for them and was unable to find them, so I think that someone else must have reported them and they were caught. I was happy they were no longer on the corner with their buckets. However, I often wondered what they were up to now.

For quite some time I didn't ride the street car to my mother's house because of the water incident. Now I asked my husband to drive me there and pick me up also. He never complained. He drove me to my mother's house and would come back and pick me up to take me home. He always was good to me and for me.

My mother Helena, and her second husband Witold, on their wedding day.

When life hands you lemons…make lemon bars.

LEMON BARS
Ingredients:

1 Cup Flour
¼ Cup Powdered Sugar
½ Cup Butter
¼ Cup Nuts, finely chopped (optional)
2 Eggs
1 Cup Sugar
Dash of Salt
3 tbsp. Lemon Juice
½ tsp. Baking Powder

Mix flour, powdered sugar and butter, plus nuts if desired. Press into an 8" X 8" pan.
Bake at 350 degrees for 20 minutes.
While crust is baking, mix eggs, sugar, salt, lemon juice and baking powder.
When crust is done, immediately pour mixture into pan and return to oven for an additional 25 minutes.
Remove from oven and sprinkle with powdered sugar.
Let cool for 10 minutes before cutting.

19

About a year after we were married, my father passed away. I was devastated with the loss and insisted that Johnny handle the funeral so that every thing would be perfect for him. The funeral was perfect and I couldn't have asked for a better send off for my father. He was buried at the opposite end of the family plot from our dear Ga.

Now, my mother was all alone in the big house on Ashland Avenue. It was much too big for her alone and she no longer wanted to keep up such a big place, but she didn't know what to do. We told her to not make any big decisions right away and she agreed. It was now more important than ever that I visit her on a regular basis. I was so afraid that she would be lonely.

Within a year after that, a man that she had known nearly all her life asked her to marry him. She cared for him a great deal and wanted to be with someone in her old age, but she would not commit until she talked to her children. We all wanted her to be happy and agreed with the proposal. Soon after she sold her house and moved into a smaller bungalow in Chicago with her new husband, Witold.

One night, a few years after they were married, my brother invited my mother and Witold over to their house for dinner. Johnny and I were invited too. After dinner, the men went into the living room to talk while the ladies stayed in the kitchen. All of a sudden there was a commotion in the living room and we ran in there to find that Witold was feeling sick and wanted to go to the hospital. Ed called for an ambulance to take him there. Tests were done and it was determined that Witold had a weak heart. He was advised not to do stressful physical work like mowing the lawn. My mother found that she was getting tired more often and wanted a smaller place so that she would not have so much cleaning to do. They sold the bungalow and moved into an apartment in Norridge, IL.

They were both very happy in their apartment. They were very fond of their landlord and often watched their dog for them when they had to be away. My mother was happy and I was happy for her. I continued to visit her every Saturday and I always felt welcome in her house, no matter where she lived.

Dancing can make you feel like you are on top of the world. It brought Johnny and I together, but our deep love for each other kept us together. Nevertheless, it never hurt to feel the supreme euphoria of gliding across the dance floor in his arms!

*This is such a simple dish to make, but is oh so impressive.
The best things in life often are the simple things.*

CHICKEN BREAST SUPREME
Ingredients:

4 or 5 boneless chicken breasts
½ tsp of salt
½ tsp of pepper
¼ cup of butter or margarine
1 can condensed cream of chicken soup (10 ¾ oz)
¾ cup sauterne or dry vermouth or any white wine
1 can water chestnuts (4 oz)
2 tbsp chopped green pepper

Sprinkle chicken breasts with salt and pepper—brown on all sides in butter.
Arrange chicken in ungreased 9" X 13" pan.
Stir soup into butter remaining in fry pan, then slowly add wine.
Add remaining ingredients and heat to boiling.
Pour soup mixture over chicken.
Cover and back at 350 degrees for 25 minutes.
Uncover and return to oven for an additional 35 minutes.
Serve with rice.

20

When televisions were first introduced to the public, my parents quickly bought one. Even though my mother didn't speak good English, they enjoyed watching musical shows like The Hit Parade and The Barn Dance. This was their Saturday night entertainment. At that time, most people didn't have a TV at home, but would go to bars or taverns to watch TV. Many people did not see an advantage to having a TV at home. TV's were very expensive, so it was a thrill when of Johnny's friends won a Philco TV in a raffle.

At that time, a Philco sold for about $250.00 and considering the income at the time, this was beyond many people's means. When John's friend won the TV he couldn't keep it due to restrictions on noise where he lived. John asked him if he wanted to sell it and the friend said yes. They dickered over the price for a bit until they reached an agreement at $175.00.

The TV was delivered to our house and placed on top of the buffet. Josephine immediately fell in love with the TV and spent many hours enjoying her favorite shows. It was also very convenient as John would invite his friends over to watch special presentations like sports events or boxing. He could be at home in case a call came in yet have a good time with his buddies.

In fact, this is what happened the first time he invited his friends over to watch a football game. John had a seat in the middle of the couch and his friends were all surrounding him. Just as the game started, the phone rang. George Kralik, the man who stood up for us at our wedding, was calling. At first John was relieved to hear his friend's voice thinking it was a social call, but he soon learned that George's grandmother had died and needed to be attended to. So, John left his friends to watch the game as he took care of business. He missed the entire game.

We both loved to dance and continued to do so for many years after we got married. It was not only the dancing that we loved, but also the music. One of the orchestras we liked the best was Dick Jurgen's Band. His music was smooth and low keyed. Johnny had written a song which I thought was very good. One night while at the Aragon, I walked back stage and took a copy of the song to Dick Jurgen's. I wanted to see if his band would play the song. He accepted the copy of the song and thanked me, but he never did play it. We were surprised years later however, when we were at the Willowbrook Ballroom dancing to the music of Barron Elliot. As we waltzed around the room Johnny stopped in his tracks when it dawned on him that Barron was playing his song, the "Swing Waltz." It was a song about how he loved to swing but his girl liked to waltz, so when they danced together they did the swing waltz.

My husband and I danced very well together and decided to enter a dance competition. The Harvest Moon Festival, sponsored by the Chicago Sun Times, seemed like the best competition to start with since it was strictly for amateurs, so we entered. At first I didn't want to because I wasn't sure that we could dance well enough. However, my husband, who has always had a competitive spirit thought it would be fun, so we started to practice for the event. To my amazement, we won a few competitions and actually got as far as the semi-finals at the Chicago Stadium.

I was very lucky I found such a good man to fall in love with. We were made for each other. I was taught from the very beginning that the business was important and it came first. I was terribly afraid of the dead when I first married Johnny, however, as time when by I got over this fear. I more or less needed to get rid of this fear because there were many times when I was left alone at home and a dead body was brought in. I was learning the business quickly. I couldn't allow myself to be afraid.

I decided I wanted to help my husband with his business. There was a problem though. At home I spoke Polish, my parent's native tongue. Johnny was Bohemian and much of his work was dealing with fellow Bohemians. Johnny spoke Bohemian perfectly, but although Bohemian was similar to Polish, I didn't always understand the conversations he had with the bereaved.

The best solution was to go to a nearby high school that offered Bohemian classes to learn my husband's native language. I sat in a class with young people and really needed to listen and learn. We had a very good teacher named Mrs. Duda who helped me a great deal. She realized it was hard for me to be with all the young children in her class. So, she spent a lot of time with me after class to make sure that I was learning everything I needed to learn.

I learned quickly and if a Bohemian person came into the office and I was alone, I tried my best to understand. The classes seemed to work and I was very glad I had taken them.

Isn't it funny that when we act like a nut, everyone remembers and it becomes legend. Well, my Nut Balls are legend and everyone loves them!

NUT BALLS
Ingredients:

2/3 Cup Butter
1 Cup Walnuts (ground)
1 Cup sifted Flour
3 tbsp. Sugar
Confectioner's Sugar

Cream butter—add walnuts, flour and sugar.
Work mixture with fingers until well blended.
Pinch off bits of dough and roll into balls the size of large marbles.
Bake on lightly greased cookie sheet at 375 degrees for 10 minutes.
While hot, roll in confectioner's sugar.

21

Now I was ready to help out wherever I was needed in the funeral home. One of my main responsibilities in helping my husband in the funeral business was to take care of the women. Whenever a girl or woman was brought into the funeral home and the family came in to make the arrangements, my husband, the funeral director, would ask them for a picture of the deceased. This picture was given to me and it was up to me to dress her hair accordingly. Her hair was shampooed and then I would put it up in curlers. The hair dried overnight and the following morning I would take out the bobby pins and curlers and I'd comb the hair and arrange it according to the picture given to me. When the family came in the following morning to view her, I'd be very pleased when they were happy with her appearance. I couldn't believe that I, who was so afraid of the dead, was now left alone in the embalming room dressing the deceased's hair!

I also learned how to print the memorial folders. Every time we had a funeral, it was necessary for Johnny to drive several miles to the printer to pick up the memorial folders. Many times Johnny just didn't have the time to do all that was expected of him and so I told him that if we purchased a printing press, I'd print the folders and Mass cards. This would save him a lot of time.

So, Johnny and I and his uncle, who was a printer, decided we'd check to see if there were any printing presses on the market. We found one to our liking and Johnny's uncle checked it out to see if it would be good for me. It was and he told me he'd come over and teach me how to use it. He did and I became a printer. This job saved Johnny a lot of time. He no longer had to travel to the printer to pick up these folders. It also helped him to have more time with the families when they came in to view the body.

We always had burial or mass cards located next to the register. These were optional and made at the request of the family. The form of the card depended on the religion of the deceased. Catholics had Mass cards and Protestants had Burial cards. When someone signed the register and wanted to have a card for remembrance, they helped themselves.

At this time, I honestly didn't have time to spend on myself. Either I was cleaning downstairs, dressing hair or printing memorial folders. Upstairs I would be cooking and helping to take care of the house. Of course, Johnny's mother,

Josephine, was a godsend. She did most of the shopping, a lot of the cooking and still managed to find time to also help out in the office of the funeral home.

Being married to a funeral director, I was left alone with a dead person many times. When the police would deliver a dead person to our chapel, and Johnny and his mother weren't home, I'd have to tell the officers where to place the body and have them give me the papers showing who was brought in and how he or she died. I was then alone with a dead body in the morgue. I would be afraid. As time went on, I got over being truly afraid. There was no reason for the dead person to harm me as I wasn't harming them. The embalmer would be called and he'd come in and do what had to be done.

When John and his mother had meetings they both had to attend and we had a body in the chapel being waked, I'd stay in the office until visiting hours were over. Then I'd turn out all the lights and go upstairs and wait for Johnny or his mother to return. I wasn't afraid of being left alone upstairs.

This particular night we had a wake and it was a well known person from the neighborhood. There were a great many people coming to view him. I was alone that evening and I was in the office all night long and I was getting very tired. Visiting hours had ended so I thought I'd go upstairs and get ready for bed. It was getting late and Johnny and his mother would be home soon.

I went upstairs into our apartment. I went into the closet in our bedroom where I had my night gown hanging on a hanger and decided to change into it. I started to take off my dress when I heard a squeak in the floor and it seemed to me that someone was upstairs. I was truly afraid to move! I thought "Johnny, hurry home, please hurry home". It was now about 15 minutes after 10 p.m. and the visitors were all gone from the chapel so who was in my room? I just stood quietly and I was truly afraid. I couldn't wait until Johnny or his mother returned from their meetings. After what seemed like an eternity I decided that no one was there and started to leave the closet. Just then, I heard the floor squeak again. I was truly frightened as I thought who ever it was knew where I was and that I was planning to come out.

Johnny came home first. He walked upstairs and called to me. I didn't answer and so he called again. I was too afraid to answer. I was in the bedroom closet partly undressed. Johnny walked into the kitchen and called again. I finally answered. He heard me and asked where I was. I told him. He came into the closet and asked why I didn't turn out the lights in the chapel and why I didn't lock the door to our apartment. I told him "I was afraid". He asked "What are you afraid of"? "I assure you the person in the casket will not come up after you, however a visitor can do just that so be sure you always lock the door when you come upstairs." I'll never forget that night. I always locked the door when I entered our apartment.

This story has become somewhat of a family joke. As it turned out, I was making the noise that I was hearing. The floorboards in the closet would squeak every time I moved. I was holed up in that airless closet for at least an hour waiting for Johnny to come home and it was for naught. I didn't realize that this was the cause of the noise until later and when I did, I could help but laugh at myself and how silly I was.

Years ago, when I was still a child, I remember when a neighborhood girlfriend died and was waked at a local funeral home. My family went to the funeral home to view her. I didn't go inside because I was afraid. However, as I grew older, I got over that fear. We all change with time, for now I was no longer afraid to be left alone all by myself with a dead person!

Johnny and I with our son Bud

Johnny's mother, Josephine, loved tripe soup, but this type of soup doesn't smell so good when it is cooking. It is one of those things that can smell bad, but taste quite good. So, I guess you could say that we shouldn't always be led by our noses because we just might miss some of the best things in life.

DRSTKOVA POLEVKA (Tripe Soup)
Ingredients:

1 lb. tripe
5 oz. smoked meat
4 tablespoon flour
1 carrot
1 clove garlic
celery root
pinch pepper
pinch marjoram
pinch ginger
parsley
salt—butter

Wash tripe well in cold water, cook 1/2 hour, wash again.
In fresh cold water add salt, roots, carrot, parsley and celery cut in circles.
Ad smoked meat and tripe, cook until tender.
Cut up tripe in small noodles and cut meat in small pieces—set aside.
In a pan, add flour to melted butter and cook until flour is browned.
Put soup into browned flour stirring constantly.
Add mashed garlic, pepper, marjoram, chopped parsley, ginger.
Cook well. Add tripe and meat. Serve.

22

As we settled into married life, it seemed like we didn't go dancing as much as before. We were very content some nights to just stay home and be with each other. John was a very good piano player and some nights he would play for me as I lounged on the couch. We both had the feeling that all was right with the world.

Dancing less, I noticed I had put on some weight and I wasn't feeling as peppy as I used to be. I told my husband I think I better see a doctor. "Johnny," I said, "I'm not feeling good and I'm always tired." He agreed that I should see a doctor and insisted I go the next day and that he would drive me.

When I went to the doctor, he checked me and told me I was pregnant. We were so happy, as my husband and I both wanted a baby. We told my mother and Johnny's mother right away. They were very happy for us and we set our sites on the upcoming birth of our first child.

On the 26th of August, 1952, Johnny and I went to a neighborhood dance. It was held at the Sokol Hall, 2 doors away from our place of business. We met many of our friends there. The music was good and so Johnny and I got out on the floor and danced immediately. I was very pregnant, but that didn't stop us from enjoying ourselves. We danced and danced, along with many of our friends.

In the basement of the hall, food was being served. Since we didn't eat at home, I asked Johnny if he'd take me downstairs for a snack. He agreed. He had some tripe soup and I ordered a warm potato pancake. We ate our food and then returned upstairs to be with our friends. Johnny asked a lady friend to dance the next dance. She quickly accepted. Johnny was an excellent dancer. I sat at the table and talked with the men and women seated with us. Johnny asked me to dance, however, this time I turned him down. He couldn't understand "why". I told him I wasn't feeling well. He asked if I wanted to leave and I told him that since the music was so good, and we were with friends, we could stay awhile. However, I still wasn't feeling any better as time went on.

I then motioned to Johnny to come to me and I told him how I was still feeling. I told him I was getting sharp pains in my stomach. We stayed for about another hour before I told Johnny we should leave. As we were getting ready to leave, I told my husband that it would be a good idea to bring his mother home something to eat. So he went downstairs and bought her some tripe soup.

When we got home, his mother was very happy to receive the soup. She hadn't made tripe soup for a long time. She warmed up the soup and enjoyed it very much. Johnny was happy that his mother was pleased.

I immediately walked to our bedroom and sat down in our soft chair. Johnny went to change into his night clothes. When he returned, he asked why I hadn't changed into my night shirt. I told him I was very tired and I still wasn't feeling well. The pain in my stomach was getting stronger. He immediately called the doctor and told him that I wasn't feeling well and the doctor told Johnny to get me to the hospital and that he would meet us there. I was very naïve about the process of childbirth and hadn't realized that I was in true labor.

Johnny drove me to the hospital and then helped me out of the car when we arrived. A nurse immediately met us with a wheel chair and I could see my doctor just inside the doors of the hospital. The nurse then whisked me away to the maternity ward leaving my husband standing in the lobby feeling a little bewildered.

The night that I went to the hospital to have my first child is one I'll never forget. The pain was getting stronger and more frequent. I was laying in bed a short time when another woman was brought in and placed in the bed next to me. Oh how she hollered. I'll never forget her screaming. I asked if this was her first child and she answered, "No, I already have four and this will be my fifth!" I began to think to myself that if she's so afraid after having four children, what will it be like for me having my first?

I was given a pill by the nurse and in a short time I was fast asleep. When I awoke, I noticed that the stomach pain wasn't as strong as before I went to sleep. But, I did feel very different and had an urge to push. I called the nurse who called the doctor and soon after gave birth to a baby boy—our first child, our first son. I was so relieved to be out of pain.

I was so very happy it was a boy because that was what Johnny had wished for. Our son was wrapped in several blankets and given to me to hold. I held him and kissed him. Once I had completed the recovery period, the nurse wanted to transfer me to from the delivery area to the maternity ward. The nurse helped me to get into a wheelchair to take me to my room. Johnny was waiting in the hallway just outside the door. At that time husbands were not allowed to be a part of the birthing process and spent their time in a waiting room wondering what was happening in the delivery room.

As soon as I saw him I said, "Johnny, it's a boy! It's just as you wanted."

He smiled. He was happy. He looked at our son and said, "I'm so happy it's a boy and now we must think of what we'll name him."

"That's not a problem. We'll name him John, after you and your father and we'll call him Bud or Buddy, just as your father and you have been called many times." John kissed me and walked along side as we went to the ward.

He returned home to tell "grandma" Josephine what we had named our son. She was very happy we named him John. We were so happy to have a male child and heir to the family name.

He was a joy to us. John's mother Josephine enjoyed our son too. Many times she would take him out in the buggy and walk with him around the neighborhood. She would show him off. She was so very proud of her little grandson.

She was a great help to us. She would take care of the business for Johnny when he wasn't home and she also looked over our new son when we were out somewhere. Josephine always told us, "Go when you can because someday you may not be able to."

An Athlon Philoi outing at Fox River Grove
Bud is in the stroller that I am holding on to.

As my story progresses, we find ourselves blessed with children. While the saying goes, "As American as motherhood and apple pie"…well I always thought if it as American as motherhood and chocolate chip cookies. Cookies can put a smile on any child's face and a happy child means a happy mom.

CHOCOLATE CHIP COOKIES
In Memory of Florence Slansky

Ingredients:

1 Cup Shortening
¾ Cup White Sugar
¾ Cup Brown Sugar
2 Eggs (beaten)
1 tsp. Baking Soda
1 tsp. Vanilla
2 ½ Cups Unsifted Flour
1 tsp. Salt
1 Pkg. Chocolate Chips
1 Cup Nuts (ground)

Mix shortening, white sugar and brown sugar.
Dissolve baking soda in 2 tbsp of boiling water.
Add eggs, baking soda and vanilla mixing well.
Add salt and flour—gradually until mixed in.
Add chocolate chips and nuts.

On un-greased cookie sheet, drop tablespoons of mixture until you have 12 cookies.

Bake at 350 degrees for 10 minutes.

23

During our early married life, we became very unhappy when we heard the news that the Trianon was sold and there would no longer be dancing there. It was 1954 and our son was two years old at the time. I was back in top dancing form by then and the Trianon was close to our house so it was easy to get there.

The Aragon had changed also. The Aragon at that time was having problems. Too many other functions were taking place there besides dancing. There were prize fights held there, wrestling matches, etc. The crowd that used to go there (mainly all white male and females) was now mostly males. Times change everything! The Tuesday night dancing had stopped.

Fortunately, my husband and I continued our membership with the Athlon Philoi Club. Athlon Philoi means "prized friendship" and it held true to its name. We would meet once a month and plan things to do and places to visit. We met at a nearby community house so that it wasn't difficult for anyone to attend. At each meeting one woman was asked to bring a sweet refreshment, either home baked or store bought. Coffee was made in a huge pot and after the short meeting we'd all sit in a circle and enjoy coffee and sweets.

The children were given milk and cookies. Children were always invited and they were happy to see their friends. They spent most of their time just running around and having pure fun. We were all comfortable with this arrangement however, new rules were being made at the club house and we were told we could no longer bring the children.

We needed to find a new place and we did. We made arrangements with a new community house that had just been built and opened. We met every month just as before however, this was much better for us because we met in the club house and the children played outdoors with each other at the playground.

This went on for several months and then it was suggested that it would be best to meet at each others houses. We decided to meet later in the evening so that the children could be put to bed before anyone came for the meeting. This went on for many years until all our children were grown and then it was time for another change. After 30 years we decided to start meeting monthly at a restaurant for lunch. At first it was just the ladies who met, but when the men began to retire, they joined us too.

One of the things we planned was an annual dance. It was always held in the fall and we would sell tickets to our members as well as members of other clubs. Each member of our club was asked to sell three tickets as we needed enough people to come to cover our expenses and to come out ahead. We had to pay for the hall, the band, the printing of the tickets and all the other aspects involved in putting on a dance. The money we would make from the dance would fund our activities for the year. I don't remember any year where we didn't come out ahead after a dance.

The clubs that we sold tickets to also reserved tickets for our club members to come to their dances. As it turned out, there was a dance just about every month. Because we all came to each others dances, we got to know the people in the other clubs and we were always glad to see familiar faces when we went to the dance.

Bud with Santa - Christmas 1957

When life is sweet, a nice sweet dish is just what you need to celebrate the happiness and feeling that life is grand. What is sweeter that an apple sprinkled with sugar… maybe the apple of ones eye?

APPLE PUFFED PANCAKES
Ingredients:

6 Eggs
1 ½ Cups Milk
1 Cup Flour
3 tbsp. Sugar
1 tsp. Vanilla
½ tsp. Salt
¼ tsp. Cinnamon
½ Cup Butter
2 Apples (peeled and thinly sliced)
2 to 3 tbsp. Brown Sugar

Preheat oven to 425 degrees

Mix eggs, milk, flour, sugar, vanilla, salt, cinnamon in blender.
Melt butter in 12" porcelain quiche dish or 9" X 13" pan in oven.
Add apple slices to pan and return to oven until butter sizzles.
Do not let brown.
Remove dish from oven and pour batter over apples.
Sprinkle with brown sugar.
Bake in middle of oven 20 minutes or until puffed and brown.
Serve hot.

Serves up to 8 people.

24

Bud was a healthy, happy baby and grew quickly. Before long he was ready to enter kindergarten. He enjoyed going to school in Chicago and had many friends. Grandma or I would walk with him every morning and afternoon to school. He had to cross busy streets to get there. Soon the neighborhood began to change. Children from other neighborhoods were being bused in and as a result the district lines were changed. We were now in a different district and Bud had to change schools. It was actually better for all of us because he no longer had a busy intersection to cross and now could go walking to school by himself. He liked this.

Now that he walked to and from school by himself, his grandmother would watch him until he was in front of the school in the morning and wait outdoors for him to return in the afternoon. He loved her and she loved him. He always gave her a hug and kiss when he left home for school and also when he returned from school.

We knew that with the start of the school year, that Thanksgiving was not far off. This was a day when we always ate too much. I always insisted that we spend the day with my mother. She made traditional dishes that were very good and she always cooked in abundance. Johnny's mother would have to stay behind to answer the phone in case someone died. I felt bad that we couldn't all spend the holiday together, but someone had to mind the business. My mother would pack up a full meal that we would take home to Josephine each year. While she wasn't able to participate in the spirit of the occasion, she could participate in the eating.

My husband was and still is a very good and generous man, not only with his mother and me, but with his children too. When we lived on Lawndale Avenue, each year our Christmas tree was put up and decorated a few days before the holiday after Bud went to bed for the night. In the morning he'd go to where the tree was and call out to everyone to come and see it. The joy and wonder showed on his face.

Once the tree was put up, it was Bud's job to put up the train. I helped him do that and after it was up, he and his dad ran it. He loved playing with the train. His dad told him to be careful and when he grows older he could someday show his children how to run the train. The train was just as important to him as the Christmas tree was.

On Christmas morning, we would exchange gifts. Bud would show how happy he was with the presents he received by going around the room and kissing everyone. He would start by kissing his grandma and showing her his present, then on to his dad and finally me. I would always give him a big kiss back.

I was so pleased he was happy with the train and gifts that he received. I was especially pleased that all was going according to plan. Then, we found that Santa had left something for grandma, dad and me. After we opened our gifts we all sat around the Christmas tree and sang some Christmas songs. This was a very happy time for all.

As it was late and we had all had a full day, we put our Bud to bed so that he could wake up fresh the next morning when he'd go to church. He needed to get up early so he could look at the tree again, have breakfast and then dress himself. Dad drove him to Sunday school at church. He enjoyed Sunday school. Many of his friends were in it too. After an hour, the class came to an end and everyone was ready to return home and play with their Christmas toys.

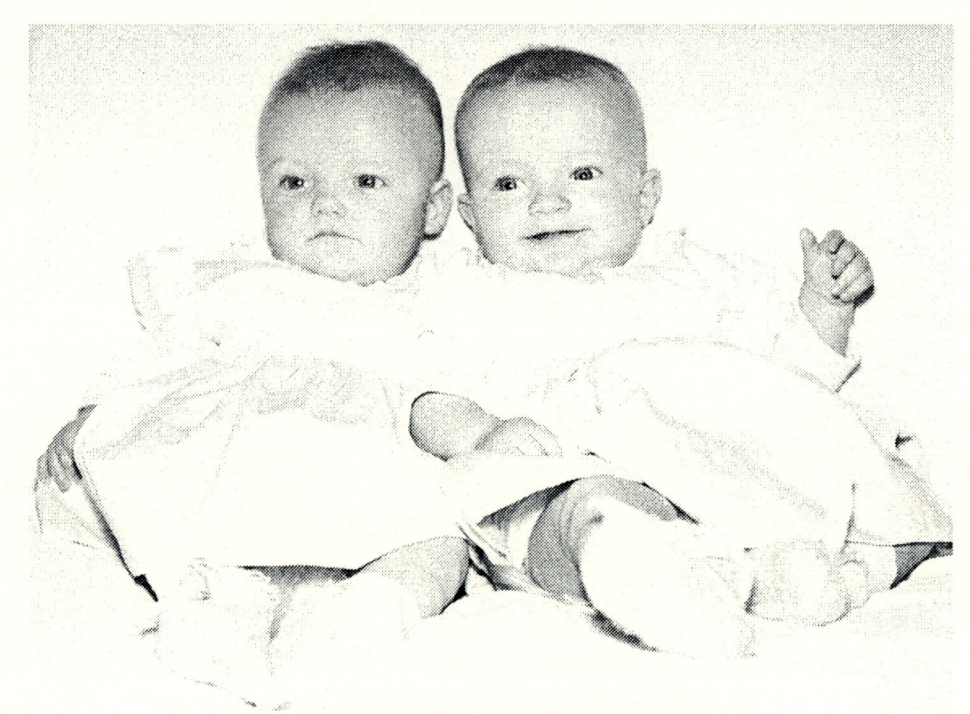

**Jane and Joan
Our daughters**

*Pierogi is one of those foods that can be made in a variety of ways. They can be filled with potatoes, cheese, sauerkraut or a combination of things. This recipe combines **two** very different ingredients that blend together to make a delicious side dish. In my life, the number **two** took on a new meaning and became the main event.*

PIEROGI FILLED WITH SAUERKRAUT AND MUSHROOMS
(Pierogi z Kiszonej Kapusty)

For the dough:
1 ¼ C flour
1 egg
salt
warm water

For the filling:
1 lb. sauerkraut
4 T. butter
1 onion
4 oz. fresh mushrooms
sour cream to serve

To make the dough, sift the flour, add the egg, salt and sufficient warm water to make a loose dough which holds in shape.
Divide the dough into quarters and roll out thinly.
Cut out circles 8.5cm in diameter.

To make the filling, chop the sauerkraut finely and saute in 3 tbsp of butter.
Chop the onion and fry in 1 tbsp of butter.
Dice the mushrooms and fry in remaining butter. Mix everything together. Place a heaped tablespoon of filling on each circle, fold over and press the edges firmly together to prevent them from opening while cooking. They should be well filled.

Bring some salted water to boil and drop the pierogi (a few at a time). When they rise to the surface, turn the heat down and simmer for 5 minutes.
Drain and serve with sour cream.

Serves 8.

25

John and I were able to take care of our funeral business, while grandmother took care of Bud. It was an ideal situation. Buddy was a healthy baby boy. He was now 5 years old and we decided this would be a good time to have another child for him to play with.

When I first suspected I was pregnant, I went to the doctor and he confirmed that I was with child. I continued to see the doctor and it wasn't long before he told me that I was most likely pregnant with more than one child. I was getting exceptionally large in the stomach area. The doctor said that I should have x-rays taken of my abdomen. I did and when he saw the x-rays, he told me that I was definitely having twins.

I wasn't surprised by this as I had twin brothers and twins ran in our family, but I was worried because my weight was so high. The doctor told me not to worry and that every thing would be just fine. However, I should continue to take daily walks and eat sensibly. I did eat sensibly, but I continued to put on a lot of weight.

You can't imagine my delight when Joan and Jane were born on May 23rd, 1957. Joan was the first born and she was beautiful. After she was cleaned up a bit and wrapped in a warm blanket, the nurse took her out in the hall to see Johnny and then to the nursery. Jane was born just a few minutes after Joan and though they looked nothing like each other, Jane was just as beautiful. They both had low birth weights, but Joan was able to leave the hospital a week after she was born. I was very sad to have to leave Jane in the hospital until she had put on more weight and was stronger. I wanted us all to be together even if that meant the Joan and I had to stay longer in the hospital, but in the end there was nothing I could do. Johnny came to the hospital and packed up Joan and took her home where he cared for her with grandma's help. I stayed at the hospital so I could be with Jane, feed her and take care of her. Every day I asked the doctor if she could go home, but the answer, was always no. I could feel that Jane was getting stronger and could see that she was gaining weight. I told our doctor, Dr. Just, that I would take good care of her at home, but he said she still needed more time.

Finally the day came when I asked the question and the answer was yes, I could take her home. I was so happy. I promised that I would feed her on schedule and take very good care of her with the help of her grandmother and her father. I wrapped her in a blanket, signed all the necessary papers and Johnny came to take us home. Grandma Josephine was just as glad as I was to have both girls home. She kissed Jane and held her tightly glowing with love for the newest addition to the family. Now there were 3 children in our family.

Grandma loved them all and was always ready to take care of them. Grandma was getting older and I didn't want her to work too hard and tried to do more myself. I helped my husband in his business and took care of our 3 children. But, I couldn't have done it all without her. She always made sure that the children were fed on time. She made delicious soups, Johnny loved her soups. While she kept up with the meals and taking care of the children, I would be downstairs in the Funeral Home dusting the office desk and chairs and opening the Chapel. Many times the floors needed to be taken care of too. I was kept very busy and I liked that.

In the afternoon, I would wash up and take our children walking. Many times we would stop at the playground. The children liked going down the slides and swinging on the swings. Oh to be young again. I watched them and wished many times to be that young and carefree again, so I could enjoy all the playground games with them. After spending a couple of hours there they would be ready to leave. When we'd arrive back at our house, Grandma always had supper cooking.

If I wasn't available to take care of our children and they cried, grandma was always near by to pick them up, rock them or feed them—she would do whatever was necessary. I know I never would have managed without her living with us. She loved her son and wanted to help as much as possible. She was a good person ready to help us all!

My brothers, John, Lou, and Ed, with me at a backyard cookout.

In this dish, the key to a wonderful meal is letting the pork simmer until tender. It takes a long time and a great deal of patience, but the wait is worth it.

FLEECKI
Ingredients:

1 Smoked Butt
Water
1 Whole Onion
1 Bag of Wide Egg Noodles
Butter

Put the smoked but in a pot and cover with water.
Bring to a boil and simmer for about one hour.
When meat is soft, remove from pot to cool off.
Cut meat into small pieces and set aside.

Bring a large pot of water to boil.
Put in whole onion (for taste) and egg noodles.
Cook according to package directions.
Drain noodles, discard onion, butter noodles and add meat.
Stir well.

Place in large serving bowl and eat, eat, eat!

26

The neighborhood where we lived, 26th Street and Lawndale in Chicago, was at one time, all Bohemian. There was the local bakery shop which carried Bohemian pastries, and the butcher shop which carried special sausages that Bohemians were familiar with. The grocery stores were also mostly owned by Bohemians. Therefore, it was truly a Bohemian neighborhood. But, as the city expanded, our Bohemian friends and neighbors began to move west and out to the western suburbs.

Johnny told me that his father died of peritonitis from a ruptured appendix. He also told me that the man, who owned their building before his dad, also died of the same illness. Now, Johnny owned the building and I was so terribly afraid that he would die early as had the other two owners.

I watched him very closely. I didn't want him to over work and I always wanted him to get enough rest. After living in the building for several years, I began to ask him to look around for another location. At first he thought I was foolish, however, as I talked to him I got him to realize it could happen to him too.

With the birth of the twins, Johnny saw that the apartment was too small and that we would need to find a larger place to live. My husband and I had the large bedroom and Josephine had the smaller bedroom. Bud had stayed with us as an infant, but he was now of an age where he needed his own room. However, we did not have bedrooms for him or the twins. What would we do?

There honestly wasn't any room to expand or add on to the building and we knew that as the children got older things would become more difficult. Additionally, it was now 1957 and so many people now had cars that it was difficult for them to find parking on the street when attending a funeral. We really needed a parking lot, but there was no available land in the area for such an improvement.

Finally, he agreed with me and started to look around for another location for his business. We looked at several places that were up for sale however none of them appealed to Johnny. We decided it would probably be best to find the right location and build a new building according to our liking. So, we began looking at empty lots that were for sale. Where would we build our new funeral home? This was the big question.

My brother Ed and his family lived in the western suburb of Westchester. This particular Sunday, they invited us to their house for an outdoor BBQ they were having. Several neighbors were also invited. We had a wonderful time talking and laughing together.

After we left Ed's house, Johnny and I drove around the business section of the town. Then Johnny needed gas for his car so we stopped at a gas station and noticed there was a "For Sale" sign on the property across the street from the gas station on 22nd street. We walked around the property and thought this would be a nice location for a funeral home. We didn't want the real estate person to know who we were and what we wanted the property for, so we asked a friend of ours who lived in Westchester, Gus Galandek, to inquire as to the price and size of that particular lot that was up for sale. After we got this information, we decided we'd try to get our money together and perhaps we could purchase it.

Then we began to visit a number of new funeral homes in the area. We would make notes about the things we liked at each one so we would have ideas when we were ready to build our own. We also were able to see the downfalls of several funeral homes and what we needed to avoid. After finishing all of our research and seeing that our dream was possible we went to talk to Johnny's mother.

Johnny's mother had some money which she agreed to loan us. We had already made up our minds that we wanted to leave the neighborhood. We now had 3 children and we wanted the best for them. We wanted better schools, etc. Johnny drove our son out to the property and they walked around it. He then asked little Johnny what he thought of it. He was so young that he didn't know what to say except that he liked what he saw.

In the evening Johnny and I would sit at the kitchen table and I'd draw what we thought we'd like in a Funeral Home with living quarters above. We wanted 3 large chapels, a large beautiful lobby, a large morgue and a showroom for caskets. By having the showroom, this would save Johnny a lot of time by being able to show the caskets to the families as they made their arrangements instead of driving out to the casket showroom which was several miles away. This proved to be a very good idea. After we built our showroom, many funeral directors came to see our place and all commented what a good idea this was.

I started to draw pictures as to what we wanted and many times I'd erase parts of what I drew and often I'd start all over. Johnny would always be walking around with a tape measure so he could determine what actually sizes would be and how wide doorways would need to be. We finally, became sure of how we wanted everything laid out and I was able to draw the final picture.

We found an architect, called him, and showed him what we wanted. He said he would draw up some pictures and we could come back and look at them and see if he had captured what we really wanted. After three different drawings that we changed, he made out the plans exactly to our specifications. Johnny spent several hours consulting with him to make sure that he knew about the things that were needed that weren't on our simple drawing. After two months, the architect called us when the blueprints were finished and we were very happy with his work.

After the plans were completed, we contacted a builder and showed the blueprint to him. We asked him what he would charge and after some negotiations, we finally came to an agreement even though the amount was more than we had thought it would be. Then, my husband showed him the type of brick he wanted for the building. The builder told us he could start immediately and he ordered the brick which arrived in a few days. It wasn't long before the building of our new funeral home began. We were all happy and excited. Johnny and I would drive out to Westchester several times each week to watch the progress on the building. It was a good thing because at one point, the brick changed colors half way up an exterior wall. Johnny made them take all the brick down and do it over again so it matched. It took 14 months for the building to be finished, but in the end it was beautiful and everything we hoped it would be.

Once the building was finished, we contacted an interior designer to help us furnish and decorate the inside. We told her what we wanted and she told us what would be nice. We liked her advice as to the general color scheme and the furniture. We picked out the paint colors and the carpeting while the finishing touches were added. Then we selected draperies, chair cushion and couch material to complement the walls and carpeting. She knew exactly what we wanted and we got along with her very well. When it came to buying the furniture for the funeral home lobby, we found the exact style we liked, but not in the color we needed. We ended up buying the furniture and having it all recovered in a fabric that matched our color scheme of beige and brown. The furniture turned out beautiful.

Johnny and Bud
Breaking ground for our new Funeral Home
in Westchester

Moving can be so sweet, yet so sad. You catch yourself looking forward to new beginnings, yet not quite ready to let go of the cherished past.

BUTTERBALL COOKIES
Ingredients:

1 Cup Butter
4 tsp. Powdered Sugar
1 tsp. Vanilla
2 Cups Flour
1 Cup Nuts (chopped)

Cream but and sugar until light and fluffy.
Add vanilla.
Gradually add flour.
Mix well.
Fold in nuts.
Shape into small balls and place on un-greased cookie sheet
Bake at 350 degrees for 18 minutes.
Role in powdered sugar while hot.

Makes 3 dozen

27

We began looking over our belongings deciding what we would take with us and what we would leave behind. These were difficult decisions to make. We took our dining room furniture (which we still have to this day) and all of our knick knacks. However, we left many beautiful things behind, including oriental rugs and some other beautiful furniture.

Grandma Josephine decided to stay in the city above our old funeral home until the building was sold. Her sister, Toni, came to live with her during this time of transition so that she wouldn't be alone. The place eventually was sold, but the new owners didn't keep it as a funeral home. When the sale was completed Josephine moved in with us and her sister, Toni, went back to live with her son. I'm sure that this arrangement was a nice change of pace for both of them.

In the winter of 1957, we moved into our "Budilovsky Westchester Funeral Home." Our new apartment above the funeral chapel had 6 rooms. It had a very large parlor, dining room and then sliding doors leading into the kitchen. The kitchen was large and light. There were 3 windows on the north side of the kitchen above the sink area. The first thing we did was to purchase a new kitchen set which now had 6 chairs instead of 3. Even though the twins were too young to sit in a chair, I was looking toward the future and wanted everyone to have their own chair. I knew it would not be long before they would be out of their high chairs and joining us at the table. It seemed like I blinked once between the time Bud was in a high chair and the day he refused to sit in it anymore.

I wanted new furniture for our living room and Johnny agreed, so we purchased a curved sofa for a corner section of the parlor and a large long sofa to be placed in front of the windows. We brought our bedroom furniture from Lawndale, but bedroom furniture for the children was purchased as needed. Once the girls outgrew their cribs, we bought them twin beds. We also purchased a twin size bed for Bud. This was a time when we had to do a lot of thinking, we didn't want to buy too much and wanted to use as much of what we already had.

Then we purchased a new TV and two occasional chairs which we placed opposite the TV. We also brought our organ from the old place and placed that in our parlor. Once everything was in place, we brought Grandma Josephine over to see it. She was very pleased with everything. Immediately we extended an invitation for her to come live with us, but she wasn't quite ready to move and wanted to stay at the old place until it sold. She also said that she wanted to bring quite a few things from the old place and was worried there wouldn't be enough room. We assured her she could bring whatever she wanted and we would make room for it. We loved the new place.

We put up signs that showed we were open for business and we even put a newspaper advertisement in the local papers stating our opening date. We held an open house where we invited close friends and relatives to help us show off our new facilities. Many of our new neighbors in Westchester came to look over our place.

We invited all the people who had been helping us show off our place to have dinner with us. We made arrangements with a local Bohemian restaurant and celebrated the start of this new phase of our life.

While our old funeral home was called Budilovsky's Funeral Home, we decided it would be best to call our new funeral home, Budilovsky Westchester Funeral Home. There were no other funeral homes in the town so it was an appropriate name. The sign and advertising said, "John A. Budilovsky—Westchester Funeral Home." In other words, John's name was above the name of the funeral home—star billing.

We were constantly complimented on how well our new place looked. This was a busy and happy time of our lives. Within a short time we received our first call. A neighbor passed away and the family asked if we would handle his burial.

Our family standing outside the Westchester Funeral Home
Bud, Jane, Me, Joan and Johnny

There are times in life when you feel pulled in two different directions…our first years in Westchester I often felt that way. What a relief to have a slice of no pull strudel or fruit coffee cake after a day of having a twin in each arm while answering the door to the funeral home…oops! Not enough hands.

NO PULL APPLE STRUDEL
Ingredients for dough:

2 Cups Flour
¼ lb. of Butter
½ Cup Milk (scalded)
1 Egg Yolk

Preheat oven to 350 degrees
Scald milk with butter.
Mix in flour and egg yolk.
Pour into 9" X 13" pan.
Place in oven while you peel and slice the apples.

Ingredients for filling:

Apples
Vanilla Wafers
Raisins
¼ lb. Butter
Sugar
Cinnamon

In sauce pan, melt butter.
Add apple slices, crushed vanilla wafers, raisins, sugar and cinnamon.
Mix well.
Remove dough from oven. Spread filling over dough.

Bake for 45 minutes to 1 hour.

28

When we moved into our new house in Westchester we were happy. Bud would go to the local school which was not too far away from the house. He was picked up by a school bus and brought home by bus too. There was another young boy living further down the block who rode the bus with our son. His name was Phillip Hauer. He would come to our apartment many times just to talk and play with our son. He was a good boy and polite too. We felt our son could learn from him. Those years quickly flew by.

When we first moved to Westchester, the girls were six months old and were in the house all day long. Johnny often was in Lawndale at the other funeral home as the business there was as brisk as usual. When the bell rang for the Westchester funeral home, I would put a baby in each arm and go downstairs to help the customer and begin the process for the funeral, leaving the bulk of the work for Johnny when he returned. There were times when the bell rang in the middle of a feeding or changing a dirty diaper, but we got everything handled quickly and answered the door as soon as possible.

The girls were good and were soon used to coming down to the office with me. It seemed like in just a short time they were crawling and then walking. And eventually I potty trained them. They kept me busy.

My brother, Ed, lived nearby and he came over frequently to ask if I needed anything from the store. He knew Johnny was at our other funeral home most of the day and I didn't drive, so he'd purchase whatever I needed. He was good to me.

Johnny and I got along beautifully. I honestly loved my husband and I believe that he loved me. It was very easy for us to show our affection for each other and we would always kiss or hug when we saw each other. No matter what was happening in our life we were happy simply because we were together. Now, for the first time in our marriage, Johnny would be away from home for long hours and I really missed him.

There were times when I would want to go out to eat and Johnny always asked me where I wanted to go and then he would take me there. Many times we asked John's mother, Josephine, to go out to eat with us and she always did. She enjoyed eating out too. It made her happy that we wanted her to come with us. She did so much for us and this was just a little thing we could do for her.

Two years after we moved in to our new house, the old Funeral Home was finally sold. It was purchased by a man who wanted to turn it into a church. He insisted that many things be left behind as a condition of the sale. It broke our hearts to leave the beautiful Persian rugs and an old clock in the kitchen, but we felt we had little choice. For all the worrying that Josephine did about her belongings being accommodated in the new house, she ended up bringing far less than she thought she would.

Josephine soon moved in with us, bringing her old bedroom set. Our house had three bedrooms. Johnny and I shared one, the twins another and Bud the third. We had to make some changes to accommodate grandma and Bud was the one who ended up giving up his bedroom. We moved his single bed, small desk and dresser to a small room off the kitchen. He was delighted as we told him he could decorate the room as he wished. He carefully put pictures up around the room and arranged the furniture just the way he wanted. At about this same time, Bud was also starting to take an interest in hobbies. As such, he was also given a room near the garage where he would have ample space to make model airplanes and do the things he wanted.

Over the years, things had not changed much when it came to the business and our personal affairs. It would happen from time to time that we would receive a call just as we were about to step out the door for an event. Whenever there was a special occasion like a wedding, graduation or anniversary, Johnny would try to work his schedule out so that he could take me there, drop me off and return to his work. In most cases he was able to pick me up, but when he couldn't I would find someone to drive me home. If it was not a special occasion, I usually opted to stay home. I knew there would be many other times when we could go out together and this wasn't going to be one of them.

Johnny's mother had several sisters and they were all very close. When her birthday came, Johnny and I invited all her sisters to come to our house for supper. Johnny picked up each sister and brought them to our house. His mother was very happy they all could come. I served a nice meal and at the end we had a birthday cake for her. We had her make a wish and blow out all the candles. When she blew out all the candles we congratulated her asked what she wished for. She said that if she told us she would never get her wish and so it went year after year. She never told us.

Johnny was an exceptionally good son. He always wanted to do all he could to please his mother. He was also an exceptionally good son-in-law. That not only made me happy, but my mother too.

Bud and Johnny sitting on Johnny's
1950 Pontiac with Van Auken Guards

As we melded into the non-distinct middle class of suburbia, our life seemed to lose some of the ethnicity we loved so much in the old neighborhood. The smell of kolacky baking in the kitchen would bring our heritage back to us and in that we felt security.

KOLACKY
In memory of Mrs. Slovacek

Ingredients:

4 Cups Flour
4 tsp. baking powder
4 tbsp. powdered sugar
1 tbsp. salt
4 Egg Yolks
1 lb. butter (½ pound sweet & ½ pound salted)
1 12 oz. package of cream cheese
2 Egg Whites
1 tsp. Half and Half or Cream
Fruit Filling—Apricot/Strawberry/Raspberry etc.

Using ½ pound of butter and 1 cup of flour; blend together to form stiff dough. Set aside.
Sift 3 cups of flour, baking powder, and salt together. Set aside
Using ½ pound of butter, egg yolks, cream cheese and sugar for mixture using blender.
Add flour mixture to batter slowly. Once blended, add stiff dough and mix thoroughly.
Refrigerate mixture overnight.

Beat egg whites with cream until thick. Set aside.
Roll dough out to desired thickness and cut into rounds (a small glass inverted can be used)
Using bottom of smaller glass—press indentations into dough for toppings
Brush rounds with egg and cream mixture.
Place fruit filling in indentation.
Bake at 350 degrees for 15 to 18 minutes.

29

I remember a beautiful day when the sky was blue with white clouds floating by. As I walked into the kitchen at the sink I could see for blocks far in the distance. It was a beautiful sight. There were tall trees with green leaves which turned their color to gold as time went by. We all loved our new house and the scenery was so different from the city.

Within a short time, our children met some of the neighborhood children and they got along beautifully. We were all happy with our new house and neighborhood. The children were happy and did very well in school.

Westchester was a beautiful new village and the people were exceptionally friendly. I was surprised when I found that one of our neighbors was Irene Robinson an old acquaintance I had known when we had worked together at Montgomery Ward on Chicago Avenue. She had been in the billing department at the same time I was. Since then, she married and had three children as I did. In fact, I had one son and two daughters just as she did. Our daughters became very close friends with her daughters. They played together all the time and I was pleased that they had found friends so close to the house. They walked to and from to school every day together.

My son bought a turtle for a school project when he was in the second grade. His teacher had asked each student to bring an animal to school that they would care for. No cats or dogs were allowed. They had to be small pets that could be left alone at night. She would check on their progress with the animals and give advice when necessary.

Our son did not have an animal to bring to class and so he went to the Woolworth's that was close to our house. They had a small pet section with fish, birds and turtles. Buddy decided that a turtle would be the best so he found a sales clerk, showed her how much money he had and asked if there was enough to buy a turtle and a bowl to keep it in. She told him that there was enough money to buy all that and turtle food too. He bought one of everything he needed and then hurried home to show us his purchases.

It was a very small turtle. He showed his father what he had bought and they decided to put with water in the bowl and placed a large stone in the center for times when the turtle wanted to dry off.

Johnny told Bud that he had a turtle when he was young. His father had advised him on how to take care of the animal and that the turtle should not be in the water all the time and that he needed to exercise.

We all got together and thought about a name for him. Everyone had a suggestion, but our son thought the name "Tom" would be a good one and so he was named "Tom" the turtle.

Once the school project had ended, we placed the bowl in the laundry room which became his new home. We all got used to him and loved him. We'd remove him from the water and let him walk around the laundry room. He was safe there because nobody ever entered the laundry room outside the family, who were taught to always close the door when we left the room.

As time went by, Tom got bigger and bigger. We began to feed him pieces of meat, bread and cereal along with his turtle food. Each morning, Bud would put turtle food in the bowl before he left for school. Bud enjoyed taking care of the turtle and was often found looking in the refrigerator for little treats for Tom.

As Bud got older, his interests changed and I became the main caretaker of Tom. Every morning I would give Tom a bath, scrubbing his shell to make sure it was clean. Then I would change the water in his bowl and feed him. Soon Tom was much to large for the original bowl Bud had got him and we moved him to a larger pan with a bigger rock. If it was nice outside, I would take Tom out on the porch to get some sun and exercise. He always seemed content to be out in the fresh air.

After several more years, we decided to let Tom walk freely around the laundry room. He knew that this was his home and never left the area. He was pleased to have this freedom.

One morning I woke up and found Tom lying on the kitchen floor. He had never come out to the kitchen before and I could tell that something was wrong with him. I quickly woke my husband and we called the vet. There was nothing that the vet could do for him. Tom was now gone. We all cried. We had Tom for 24 years. We buried him on the side of our house. We will always remember Tom.

Joan and Jane with Santa Claus

Family portrait - Joan, Lee, Bud, Johnny, Jane

Memories of summer getaways, memories of Christmas days…the years start to fly by season by season.

GRAPE KOLACK
Ingredients:

Several pounds of grapes (the big, seedless dark grapes)
Flour
Eggs
Baking Powder
Milk

Wash and dry grapes then put aside until dough is completed.

Dough—Mix ingredients and roll out.
After rolled, place grapes on it, sprinkle about 1 tablespoon of sugar on top.
Bake at 350 degrees for ½ hour to an hour.

BAKED LISTY
Ingredients:

½ lb. Butter or Margarine
2 Cups Flour
2 Egg Yolks
½ Cup Sour Cream
1 tsp. Vanilla
Powdered Sugar

Cream together softened butter, egg yolks, vanilla and sour cream.
Gradually add flour until to firm to use to blender. Then begin mixing remaining
flour into mixture by hand.
Place in refrigerator overnight.
Next day: Roll out until fairly thin. Cut into rectangles (about 1" by 3") twist at center and place on un-greased cookie sheet.
Bake at 350 degrees for 10 to 12 minutes (dough will remain light in color)
While still hot, sprinkle with powdered sugar.

30

A tradition that we had each Christmas Eve was that a large white laundry bag filled with Christmas gifts would suddenly appear in the family room. After supper, we'd hear bells which meant that Santa and his reindeer were near the house. The children would quickly run off to find Santa and when they went into the family room they would find the large white bag of gifts. They were always happy to find the bag, but unhappy not to have found Santa. But, their unhappiness at having missed seeing Santa would be forgotten as they were anxious to see what was inside the bag. Dad would pick out the first gift and hand it to the person whose name was on it. After that person opened their gift, more gifts would be passed out one at a time.

At some point during the gift opening process I would look out the window and exclaim that Santa was at the neighbor's house. I would call the children and they would see him too. They always wanted to go out and talk to him, however, it was very cold outdoors and I wouldn't allow them outside. Oh to be young again.

I always loved to bake and at Christmas time, after we would decorate our tree, we would invite our friends and neighbors to come over to our house where we would serve coffee and many of my homemade Christmas cookies, such as kolacky and several other kinds. They in turn would invite us into their homes as well. It would become a neighborhood tradition. One of my favorite recipes was called Grape Kolack. This has a story attached to it.

Our dear friend, Jerry Skala, bought a small farm in New Buffalo, Michigan and there was a section where he grew many grapes. When we visited Jerry and his wife, Emily, on this farm, they would always tell us that if we wanted we could pick some grapes for ourselves to take home. I'd always make sure I'd have some empty boxes or bushel baskets in the trunk of our car and the whole family would go out to the grape vines and we would fill up the boxes or bushels. This was a lot of fun and we would have a race as to who could fill their containers the fastest. When we brought the grapes home, I would start working on them. They had to be washed and dried and diced and the ones that were broken had to be thrown away.

I would then make my Grape Kolack. This was a recipe from my mother-in-law although she never really had an actual written recipe. She would remember what and how much of each item she used. I couldn't remember the ingredients as she did, so I'd look through some Czech cookbooks and make the Kolack accordingly. It was yum, yum good!

Bud, me, Jane, and Joan at the Howard Johnson Hotel pool.

Grandma Josephine made this delicious meal—it was fast and easy and everyone enjoyed it. Especially our son Bud who was growing fast and needed lots of fuel to keep his body going.

SPAGHETTI AND HAMBURGER
Ingredients:

2 lbs. of hamburger meat
1 large onion.

1 Package of Spaghetti
1 Can of Tomato Soup

Place hamburger in frying pan and start to brown. As soon as the hamburger has released some fat, add the chopped onion. Cook the hamburger with the onions until the meat is brown and the onion translucent, stirring often.

Put Spaghetti into pot filled with water. Bring to a boil and boil about 10 to 12 minutes. Drain water from spaghetti. Add meat and one can of tomato soup—stir until tomato soup has touched all spaghetti

Take out the pasta, add beans and spice, and you have Lee's variation of a fast and easy meal.

CHILI
Ingredients:

1 lb. Hamburger
1 large Onion
1 Can Tomato Soup

2 Cans Chili Beans in chili sauce
1 tbsp. Chili Powder (or more)

In frying pan, begin browning hamburger.
Add onions.
When hamburger is cooked and onions are translucent, add
Tomato soup, beans and chili powder.
Cover and let simmer.

31

Every year we took a family vacation, my husband, the children and I. We always had a wonderful time. We'd ask the children where they wanted to go and we'd listen to them all and then make a decision. Once the decision was made, Johnny would do all the planning. When the children were younger, we usually tried to stay close to home in case Johnny would be called back to prepare a wake. The kids were as happy with Elgin, Illinois as if it were a far away land. Almost every year we would spend a week in this village about 45 minutes from our home. The most important part of the vacation was the pool! The kids loved to swim and spent most of their days swimming. We would usually spend one day at an amusement park called Santa's Village. It was not far from the hotel and the kids liked the rides. We also liked to eat at the restaurant at the Howard Johnson's. Everyone in the family loved clams and they were on the menu. We ate our fill during the weeks we spent there over the years.

My husband Johnny always drove to wherever we chose to go. Once in awhile we'd take a plane. However, I always thought it was better to drive because we put everything we thought we would need in the trunk of the car. We drove to different parts of Michigan, Wisconsin and Illinois. We all learned a great deal as we visited different places of interest. Johnny would leave his mother in charge of the business when we were gone and he would call home several times a day to make sure everything was all right. If he was needed at home, we would have to cut our vacation short and return home. In that aspect he didn't like to be more than five hours away from home.

When we went traveling, and our children were very young, they enjoyed singing the Kiwanis song every time we saw a Kiwanis sign. Johnny had been a member of the Kiwanis for years and it was a big part of our life. He taught the children the song and it gave him great pleasure to hear their little voices ringing with the tune of the song. As our son grew older, he became a member of the Kiwanis...of course he already knew the song! Of course, our daughters would have liked to become members too, but the club would not allow females to join back then.

One of our favorite spots was New Buffalo, Michigan. In addition to our friends on the farm, we had several friends who had summer cottages on the lake nearby and our children loved to go swimming in the cool refreshing water. We always made sure an adult was with them when they went into the water. On our way home, we always stopped at a dinette that our friends', the Kolars, owned and they made sure our children had good meals. It was only a couple hours ride back to our house in Westchester.

When we got back, we never had trouble getting the children to go to bed. They were tired and their stomachs were full. Within an hour they were all sleeping. Johnny and I would bring in whatever we had in our car trunk. We'd take a shower and then get into bed and in no time we too were fast asleep. Of course, the next morning the children would wake refreshed and quickly inquire, as to where we would go on our next vacation.

In 1971, we heard about a new theme park that had opened in Florida. It was called Disney World and the kids really wanted to go. The girls were teenagers now and Bud was already in college. The ads on television were so appealing, we just couldn't resist going. John wanted to drive so and there would only be room for two large suitcases in the trunk. So, I packed one for Johnny and I and one for the children. Johnny was sure that we didn't have enough, but I told him that we could always buy something if we needed it.

This was the longest drive we had ever made, but the excitement kept us going. When we got there, we found a very nice motel with a swimming pool and the next day we took off for the park. My children had never been to Riverview Park which was the big amusement park of my day, but they had been to Adventureland and Santa's Village. They could not believe how big Disney World was. Of course, we had to go back again the next day because we could not see all of it the first day we visited. I was so happy to have taken my children to such a magical place. There was a part of me that wished we could have taken vacations like this when the children were younger. I knew that we were running out of time as their youth was flying by.

Our family enjoying a vacation at Santa's Village
Johnny, Joan, Bud, me and Jane

When you feed your kids beef, they will grow and grow and grow...

BAR BQ BEEF
Ingredients:

1 lb of ground beef
1 large onion—chopped
1 green pepper—chopped
1 tbsp of sugar
1 tbsp of dry mustard
1 tbsp of vinegar
1 tbsp of salt
1 cup of catsup

In a frying pan, begin to brown meat.
When it starts to release fat, add the onion and green pepper.
When meat is fully browned and onion and green pepper are soft, add remaining ingredients.
Cover and simmer for 30 minutes.
Serve on a hamburger bun.

32

Joan and Jane, our twins, are as different as night and day. Joan is very outgoing and drives a car and has many friends. Jane on the other hand is shy and has few friends. But, the friends she has truly enjoy her company and are always ready to do things with her. Jane does not drive a car although her father did try to teach her. She is afraid she may have a seizure and hurt herself and damage the car. We are very thankful that although the girls are very different in personality they are close to one another.

I also joined a local Women's Club to become friends with other women in the village. This club had several small groups within it. I joined the reading group which meant that we were asked to read a book and then give a book report on it. I enjoyed this group very much. I heard reports on the books the women read and if it interested me, I would go to the library and get that book and read it. I enjoyed reading more and more.

I also belonged to the party group. This meant we had to book a hall or restaurant when we needed to hold our next party. I enjoyed this group also very much. We booked the place and chose the menu and hoped it would please everyone.

Bud was about 8 years old at the time and we moved him into a small room off the kitchen that was very near his grandma who he loved dearly. He liked the new room and felt cozy with his bed and dresser in there.

A few years later, when he was about to graduate from high school, he had sorely outgrown the room. Bud was already over 6 feet tall and weighed 200 pounds. The little room just wasn't able to accommodate him and his things. He went to his grandma and asked her to switch rooms with him. Her bedroom set would not fit in the small room and so she demurred. We really didn't think he was serious when he asked her switch rooms, but to our dismay, Bud found a friend at school who was unhappy living at home and they decided to find an apartment to share. Bud had started working as soon as he was old enough and he was making enough money to pay his portion of the rent. Soon they were out looking at apartments and found one that they both liked. With very little fanfare, Bud moved out.

Both boys had motorcycles and they feared that they would be stolen if they left them in the parking lot. So, each night they parked their motorcycles in the living room. It is not saying much for the décor, but they were happy.

The following fall, Bud had enrolled in college and was off to Rockford, IL. We thought he was happy there, but after one year he returned home and told us he didn't want to go there any longer and wanted to transfer to another school. We couldn't understand it as he seemed to be very involved in activities at the school and it was a beautiful campus. At first, he wouldn't tell us why, but after awhile he finally told us about his roommate in the dorm.

He shared a room with another male student who constantly had his friends staying in the room. They were loud and stayed until the wee hours of the morning—so much so that Bud was not getting enough sleep and he felt like he didn't really have his own room. He had asked the school to give him another room, however, they were unable to make any changes for him. He just didn't want to go through another year like that.

To our surprise, he wanted to move back home and go to a school nearby. Johnny took Bud over to Elmhurst College and he immediately fell in love with the school. He enrolled and stayed there until he finished his undergraduate degree.

Bud had grown up quite a bit during his time on his own and his relationship with his father deepened along with his maturity. As they began to become closer, Bud talked Johnny into buying a motorcycle and riding with him. Johnny had always wanted a motorcycle since he was a youth and it didn't take much for him to be persuaded. Soon Bud and Johnny were off riding together, enjoying the open road and the thrill of the wind rushing about them.

Something to warm your tummy on a cold winter night-

LEE'S BARLEY SOUP
Ingredients:

½ lb. Chuck Meat
Water
1 Carrot—chopped
1 Onion—chopped
1 C. of Barley

Place meat in large pot.
Put enough water in the pot to cover the meat and bring to a boil.
Remove any white foam from top.
Continue to boil—add carrot, onion and barley.
Continue to boil until meat is soft. Put fork into meat to check this.
Continue to boil for about one hour.
Before serving remove meat and add about one tablespoon of sour cream.

33

Johnny and I had quickly established a social and business life in Westchester, but the thing I loved the most was living close to my brother Ed. Ed had always been good and wonderful to me. I felt close to him and his family and it gave me a sense of security to know he was so close by.

It was a very sad day when my brother told me he would be moving his family to Columbus, Ohio. He'd been working for Western Electric since graduating from college. Having worked his way up in the company he always managed to stay in Chicago. Over the past few years, he'd been offered positions that would take him away from the city where we were born and raised and he always refused the offer.

Now he was at the age and seniority where if he didn't accept the next offer, he would be stuck in his present position for the rest of his career. So when he was offered a promotion to work at the new plant that had just been built in Ohio, he talked the matter over with his wife, Lydia, and they decided they would go for it.

It seemed like they were gone in a matter of days. Their house was sold, they bought a new one in Ohio, got the children enrolled in school and himself established in his new job.

Now, I had a brother in Arizona, one in California and one in Ohio. The unfortunate thing was they all lived in lovely places I really wanted to visit, but with the business, it was just too hard to get that far away to see them.

Not long after my brother moved, my mother's second husband died. They had nearly eighteen years together and they were happy years for both of them. Again, my husband was pressed into service to prepare a funeral for my family. The funeral was set for a Saturday morning. Floral arrangements had been ordered and the funeral remembrance folders had been printed. I called all my brothers so that they could return home for the funeral while my mother was on the phone with her friends notifying them of the arrangements. He would be laid to rest next to Ga in the family plot.

Saturday arrived and the chapel was full of friends and as the music began to play, ma began to cry. It was so hard for us, her children, to see her in such distress, we began to cry also. She would be alone again.

I asked her to give up her apartment and come to live with us so she would not be alone, but she said she had a good landlord and wanted to stay. Her landlord would shop for her and she would take care of his children when he and his wife went out. I told her that the invitation was always open and that if she ever changed her mind, all she needed to do was call and we would come and get her. After all, Johnny's mother had always lived with us, it was only right that my mother also be taken care of.

I was very worried about her finances. When Witold retired from a very good job, he had the choice of taking his pension only until his death or if he preceded his spouse the pension could go on until she died. My mother told him to just take the pension until his death as it was a higher amount per month and she wanted him to be comfortable in his old age. Now that Witold was gone, his pension was also gone. My mother's income was much less now than when her husband was living.

Our teenaged daughters Jane and Joan by the
Westchester Funeral Home in front of dad's new limo

This chapter marks the finding of a nice parcel of land that became the place where we had our first house that was not a part of a funeral home. It was a big change for us, but we still had our favorite foods to keep things on an even keel.

CABBAGE PARCELS (Golabki)
Ingredients:

1 large cabbage (with big leaves)
6 oz. long grain rice
2 large onions, peeled and chopped
2 cans mushrooms or 1 lb. fresh mushrooms
1/3 C butter
1 can tomato juice, vegetable stock or mushroom stock
salt and pepper for seasoning

Slice through the base of the cabbage and cook in lightly salted boiling water until tender. When the leaves are tender, peel off. You may have to peel the first layers first and then return the cabbage to cook and continue peeling the leaves until all are done.
Boil the rice until just tender.
Drain and set aside.
Fry the onions in butter until softened.
Dice the mushrooms and fry lightly with the onions.
Mix with the rice and season well.
Place a spoonful of the rice mixture in each cabbage leaf and wrap it carefully, folding the ends under like a parcel.
Heat the oven to 400F.
Grease a roasting pan and fill it with cabbage parcels, packing them tightly together.
Pour over enough tomato juice, vegetable stock or mushroom stock to cover them.
Cover and bake in oven for 20 minutes. Remove cover and bake for another 10 minutes to brown the cabbage parcels lightly.

Serves 6.

34

In 1974 we decided to sell the funeral home in Westchester. The twins would be graduating from high school the following year and both had been planning to go to a local community college and live at home. Bud had been living away from home for a few years by this time, having graduated from college. He was now studying law at Kent University in downtown Chicago, and was living on his own. It was evident that Bud would never take over the business as he wanted to pursue a career as a lawyer. Johnny and I longed for the day when we could do what we wanted when we wanted and not have to worry about our plans being interrupted.

I was just about this time that Johnny was approached by the owners of another funeral home who wanted to buy ours. They wanted to expand their business and thought our location was suited for their needs. After much agonizing, Johnny finally agreed to sell the Funeral Home.

Now that we had decided to sell the funeral home and retire, we needed a new house. We decided to buy some property and design a house that would meet our needs. Johnny combined his love of riding his motorcycle with scouting out properties.

One day he found an area that he really liked and headed home to tell me about it. He had talked to the developer and there were two lots available in a brand new subdivision called Chambord. One lot was near the edge of the community and one was located in the center. My husband liked the lot toward the center of the subdivision and asked the salesman who had bought the lot next door. To his surprise, it was Fred Bodie, an old high school friend of his. That made the decision even easier and we bought the lot.

Before we called an architect, we decided I'd draw some pictures as to what we wanted. We had been so successful doing this with the funeral home, we wanted to plan our house the same way.

In the evening I'd take some paper, a pencil and a ruler and begin to draw what I thought would be ideal for us. Johnny would always be near by and add his thoughts. One thing that he wanted was wide hallways and the other was an office for himself. Both of which were worked into the plans. I drew and drew and finally drew something that I thought would be perfect. I showed it to my husband and he liked the drawing too.

My husband called an architect and showed him what we wanted. The architect took over. We were happy we'd have something we've wanted and the location of this building would be in a beautiful section of a new community.

Johnny's cousin, Florence, shared many wonderful recipes with us. Here's another that the kids really enjoyed. Of course they always looked forward to Florence's visits because it meant that mom would soon be cooking something really good.

PTACKY
(Pigs in Blanket)

In memory of Florence Slansky

Ingredients:

Round Steak
Flour
Salt
Pepper
Bacon
Onion
Toothpicks
Cream of Mushroom soup

Take round steak and lightly flour. Pound until thin.
Season with salt and pepper.
Cut into strips about three inches wide.
Inside each strip place a strip of bacon and a slice of onion.
Roll and fasten with toothpick.
Roll bundle in flour, place in fry pan and brown on all sides.
Will all bundles in pan, add water and simmer slowly for about 1 to 1 ½ hours.
Add cream of mushroom soup and continue to cook until soup is heated.

Serve with dumplings, noodles, rice or potatoes.

35

When my twin daughters graduated from high school, we decided it would be nice to go on a cruise to celebrate this milestone. None of us had ever been on a cruise so it was something we were all looking forward to. We looked at several vacation brochures and finally decided where we wanted to go.

We over-nighted in Florida and took a taxi the next morning to the pier. We were all very excited and happy. We boarded the ship and were given directions to our cabin. Then, we heard the ship's horn and the loud speaker announced we were about to leave. We went out on the deck and waved to the people watching from shore. This was exciting for all of us—our first cruise. We hoped that the weather would be as bright and calm as it was on our departure day. However, it didn't happen that way.

After being out on the water for a day and enjoying the sea breezes and blue skies, the sky began to get cloudy and the sun disappeared. A storm began brewing and we watched as the water became choppy and the breeze became a strong wind. We began to feel a little frightened so we got together in our room to talk and pray. Finally the thunder and lightening stopped. We felt our prayers were answered.

Then, as we entered the Bermuda Triangle, all the electricity on the ship went dead. There wasn't power anywhere on the ship and we were floating around at sea unable to steer through to our destination. The power outage lasted for several hours and the reasons the crew came up with seemed very vague and a little contrived. As night fell, we could see other cruise ships off in the distance as they passed by. Our ship did not even have emergency lights and I am sure they could not see us. I was thinking of how we could be rescued with no one able to see us and began to worry. Then, all of a sudden the lights came on and we started making our way to the next island. We were relieved to say the least. Despite the crew's assurances that it was merely a technical problem, I still think it is strange that it happened in the Bermuda Triangle.

We decided it would be best for each of us to get some sleep. We didn't know what would come up next as we sailed through the Caribbean. Thank goodness that after that storm and the power outage, there were no other problems.

The girls loved to swim and went swimming in the pool on the ship every day. The children and my husband all enjoyed the pool. It was getting late one day and I asked my husband and the children to leave the pool so we could go for supper. I imagine they were tired because they were ready to leave the pool. We all dressed and then went into the dining room. The meal was delicious. There were several choices on the menu and everyone ordered exactly what they wanted.

After we ate, we all walked around on the deck and finally went to our room and changed for bed. It was a busy day and everyone was tired. We all closed our eyes and fell asleep.

The following day we sailed to a town and we were told we could explore if we wanted. The children were ready and they wanted to see as much as possible. They also wanted to buy souvenirs. They walked with Johnny and me for a bit, but then went off by themselves for a short distance. I was truly frightened at this time. I thought, what if they get lost and can't find their way back? However, all that worry was for naught. They found us and in a short time we were all headed back to the ship.

At the next port, we decided that we would divide up into two groups. Joan and her dad would go in one direction. Jane and I would go in another. I felt much more secure with this plan than with the girls going off by themselves. As we separated, my husband called out, "Be sure to be back before the ship sails at 3:00 pm." I gave him the okay sign and proceed off the pier with Jane.

Jane and I had a wonderful day. We shopped, took pictures, looked at sights and had lunch at a local restaurant. As we were walking down a picturesque street, I looked at my watch and it was nearly 2:30 so I suggested we head back to the pier. We knew we weren't that far away and would be back with plenty of time to spare. We finally made it to the port and headed to the ship. We were talking and laughing as we went along, but when we entered the ship, nothing looked right. It was then we noticed that we were on the wrong ship. We looked across the bay and saw our ship, The Song of Norway, quite a way off at another berth. I looked at my watch and thought to myself that we would never make it that far in time. Jane and I took off running. In the end we did make it, but we were certainly exhausted after our long run. And to think I wouldn't let the children go off by themselves.

The next day, my husband and the girls put on their swim suits again and went swimming. They all loved swimming. I didn't go because I didn't want to get my hair wet and loose all my curls. I wanted to look nice when we went into the dining room or on shore.

We had a very good time on the ship. There was a beautiful floor show each night and also a room where movies were shown. There was always something to do, it just depended on what we wanted to do.

The dining room was clean and the food was always delicious. A cruise is a wonderful vacation. My husband and I have gone on several other cruises without our children. As all children do, they grow up and start taking vacations with their friends rather than their families. However, Joan continued to travel with us to this very day. She has taken trips with us to Canada, New York, California, Las Vegas, Minnesota, Wisconsin, Michigan, Poland, Czechoslovakia, Lithuania and Florida just to name a few.

Jane on her wedding day with her sister
Joan as maid of honor.

We did it all after retirement. What a wonderful time that was when we were free as birds to do whatever we wanted.

POTATO CHIP COOKIES
Ingredients:

1 lb. Butter or Margarine
1 Cup Sugar
3 ½ Cups Flour
1 Cup Potato Chips (finely crushed)
2 tsp. Vanilla

Mix sugar and butter until creamed well.
Add flour—one cup at a time—till blended
Add potato chips and vanilla and blend.

On un-greased cookie sheet, drop teaspoons full of mixture.
Bake at 350 degrees for 15 to 20 minutes or until lightly brown.

36

All our children are grown and starting to live their own lives now. Joan and Jane had gone to the local community college for two years after graduating from high school. Joan continued college at Northern Illinois University. Bud, having graduated from Kent Law School, was now attending International Law School in California.

Joan was dating a fellow named Terry DeMarco. He planned a party and invited his neighbor, Rick, who lived in the house next to his. It also happened that Joan had asked her sister Jane to come along and she did. Rick and Jane hit it off right away. During the course of the evening Rick asked Jane if she would go out with him the following night. She agreed.

They went out and talked and laughed and had a good time together. Rick asked Jane for a date for the following weekend and the weekend after that and so it went on. They realized that they liked each other very much.

Jane and I often went shopping together to Yorktown Mall which was not far from our house. One of our favorite things was to shop for awhile and then stop to have lunch at Wag's. After lunch we would be rested up enough to shop for the rest of the afternoon. We never bought all that much, but we loved looking. It was during one of our "girl" lunches that Jane told me how much she liked Rick and I knew then that they would some day get married.

Soon, they knew that they loved each other and Rick asked Jane to marry him. He was very formal about the whole thing—he came to me and to Jane's father and asked our permission to marry our daughter. We knew she loved him, so we agreed.

Jane had a large formal wedding. We pulled out all the stops for her as she was our first child to marry and we wanted so much for her to start her married life in a happy manor. Johnny proudly walked her down the aisle and her sister Joan was her maid of honor. Bud was also in the bridal party. It was such a festive occasion and one we will always remember.

When Bud was in for the wedding, he told us that his school had planned a tour of Europe and the Orient—China, Japan etc. It was essential that he go as it was on this tour that they would be exposed to the workings of international law. He would be away for an entire school year. The problem was that he needed money to pay for the trip. We agreed to pay for this vital part of his education. He dutifully wrote on a weekly basis while he was in Europe telling us about what he was learning and how much he appreciated the opportunity. With every letter we got, Johnny and I wanted more and more to visit Europe.

Now that the children were gone and the business was sold, we finally had the time to enjoy ourselves. I had always wanted to go to Europe, but we could never do that because we'd be too far away from the business. Now that we were we retired, we started making plans for a European vacation. When my brother Lou heard of our plans, he asked if he could go along with us.

My brother knew his way around Europe. He was stationed in France and central Europe while in the army and it was there that he received two Bronze Battle Stars. He had always wanted to return during peace time so that he could enjoy himself there. He was a very outgoing person so he saw all he was able to see during the war, but so much had been bombed and ruined that he wasn't able to see the beauty of it. He agreed to go to Europe with us as our tour guide. Johnny and I were really looking forward to this vacation. My brother Lou spoke many languages.

My husband and I were very happy he wanted to go with us. He told us not to pack too much as we could always buy what we needed there. We each had one suitcase. When my brother came to the house with one very small suitcase I asked if he really had everything he needed and he said he did.

He looked at our large suitcases and said, "What have you got in your suitcases? It's too much."

"Perhaps I packed too much," I told my brother. "I'd rather have too much than not enough and need to buy something. I honestly don't want to buy anything in Europe, especially clothes."

While in Europe I did however, buy several items to take home as souvenirs. We bought several wall hangings and several small items to put in our curio cabinet. They were things that would remind us of our trip.

I was so happy my brother was with us. He took us all over Germany. We ate in different German restaurants. The food was so tasty. At the end of each day, we'd return to our hotel and begin making plans for the next day.

We drove around and passed a huge department store. I asked my brother to stop so I could visit that store. Perhaps I would be able to find something to take home. My husband and brother had no desire to stop or shop, however they were all good to me and we stopped. In this department store there was a huge restaurant. We decided to have our lunch there. The lunch was wonderful and feeling refreshed, we were ready to see more.

I loved shopping and so I was happy to walk around the store and see what was available. My husband and brother left the store and sat outdoors on a long bench and watched the people as they entered and left the store. They enjoyed that and I enjoyed looking around the store to see what I could purchase to take home.

After about an hour, we got into our car, Lou sat at the wheel and we drove off. Lou asked us where we should go, but we didn't know the area so we told him to just drive around and we'd see what there was to see.

Having seen a great deal of Germany, we decided it was time to see another country. There was still so much I wanted to see. Before we left I remembered our son had a friend in France and I told my husband we should look him up. We began to drive to his house. We spent at least a half a day driving before we arrived at his place. He and his wife lived on the same property his parents lived on. His parents had a gorgeous big house and he had a similar house but much smaller. His house was located at the entrance to their property. It was a lovely section with the two houses located near each other.

We asked Bud's friend and his wife to drive with us and show us a little bit of France. They did. They decided to take us to a small café where we stopped and had some coffee. This woke us all up a bit. We were happy to have them showing us the important parts of France. We drove him and his wife back to their house and then asked how we'd get back to our hotel. He told us the best and fastest way to get to the hotel. When we arrived at our hotel, Lou parked the car and we went up to our room. We were tired and in no time at all we were fast asleep.

The next day we decided to go out and see all that we could. We decided we'd go shopping for just a short time. I wanted to find something worthwhile to take home to show our friends. After a short trip, we got back in the car and drove around the town.

Much to our sorrow, we found ourselves heading back to the Netherlands where our overseas journey had begun. We returned the rental car and got ready for our long flight home. Our European trip was spectacular and had come to an end. Soon we were back in the U.S.

A few months after returning from our trip I noticed that my mother's health was failing. I really didn't feel that she was well enough to live on her own anymore. Instead of asking her to come and live with us, this time I insisted that she come to live with us. To my surprise she did not resist all and immediately moved in. I had no idea at the time how terribly sick she was. She steadfastly refused to see a doctor and said that she was just getting old and slowing down. Finally I called the family doctor and asked him to make a house call. He came and after examining my mother he advised that she needed to go to the hospital for further testing. The testing showed that she had cancer and that it was advanced. She would not be with us much longer. Oh, how could I live with out my ma? I couldn't believe this was happening. I loved her so much and wasn't ready for her to go on to heaven.

I was grateful that I had my mother with me. She and Josephine had always been friendly with each other, but now they were becoming close. They enjoyed watching soap operas together and shared an easy companionship. These two women had been helping me and taking care of me for years and now it was my turn to take care of them. I cooked for them everyday and tried to make sure that every meal was nutritious. But, my mother began eating less and less.

Barely two years after she came to stay with us, my mother died. My husband and I were now retired from the funeral business, but you must know that he had his hand in all the arrangements for my mother who was waked at our old funeral home in Westchester. Johnny personally attended to every detail and made sure that everything was done perfectly.

After the wake and funeral, the procession headed out to the Bohemian National Cemetery and she was laid to rest between her two husbands. Years later, when my brothers were visiting the cemetery, they saw some Polish women planting flowers. As they all lived far away, they quickly conferred with each other and approached the women to see if they would plant flowers each year by my parent's headstone. The women agreed and my brothers gave them money. Although it has been 26 years since my mother's death, the women still plant flowers every year. My brother kept in contact with them sending money to pay for the flowers and for their effort. Every spring when I visit my mother's grave I am so happy to see the beautiful pansies that grow there.

My family's headstone at Bohemian National Cemetery
Listed are: Dad - Ludwik, Mother - Helen, Witold my mother's second husband and Ludwik our Ga

Not only do you need a big pot to make this stew, but you need a big family gathering to eat it. While stew always tastes better the second day, I always made sure that plenty of people where there to partake on the day it was made.

POLISH BIGOS (Hunters Stew)
Ingredients:

4 lbs sauerkraut
1 cup apple juice
1 lb smoked pork butt
1 lb spareribs
1/4 lb bacon
1 can tomato (large)
2 cups water
2 bay leaves
   black pepper
   salt
4 lbs heads of cabbage
1 lb pork loin chop or country-style pork ribs
1 lb smoked kielbasa
1/2 cup onions (chopped)
16 ounces fresh mushrooms
1 ounce mushroom (dried)
2 tablespoons flour

Brown pork and spareribs in a large heavy pot.
Add smoked butt with 1 cup of water and simmer until 1 hour.
Add the sauerkraut and one cup apple juice.
Chop the cabbage fine and add to sauerkraut.
Add lots of pepper and salt cover and simmer 1 hour.
Remove lid and keep pot on a very low simmer.
In a pan, fry bacon until crisp, then crumble into sauerkraut mixture.
Remove most of the bacon fat and fry onions and mushrooms and flour until they just brown.
Mix into sauerkraut mixture.
Cut kielbasa into slices add to sauerkraut mixture with the tomatoes.
Bring to a boil, simmer 30 minutes and serve hot.
Serve with good rye bread

Joan and Me on my 70th Birthday...
Just before the cake caught on fire!

37

As the kids were growing up, we never had enough vacations together and in 1980 we saw the opportunity to take a family vacation to the east coast. The kids were old enough to drive now and frankly to take their own vacations, but we wanted the time together.

We drove to Niagara Falls. My husband had always been fascinated with the falls and wanted a chance to see them up close. We also drove in to New York City to visit our daughter Joan who was now living and working as an actress and singer in Manhattan. We stayed with her at her beautiful apartment that she shared with her new friend, Iris Lane, on Park Avenue.

We went there for Thanksgiving for two years in a row. One year we had Thanksgiving dinner at Tavern on the Green in Central Park. The next year we dined at the Waldorf Astoria. Truly this was a great surprise because we knew how hard it was to get a reservation there. Joan had a friend who was a waiter there and he was able to make the arrangements. In both cases, the holiday was made special because we were spending it with our daughter who we truly missed and because we were able to visit with her is such wonderful places.

Joan had many friends in New York and trips to see her always involved parties, friends and a lot of fun. She has always had such a positive attitude and bubbly personality that people are drawn to her. Once they get to know her, they find out what a truly great friend she is to have.

Every year when Johnny's birthday came, I invited his cousins and closest friends to come to the house and served them cake after everyone sang happy birthday. Now he was going to have his 70th birthday and so I thought I'd have a larger group of people come to our house to be with Johnny and wish him a happy healthy birthday.

I decided to hold the party in our basement. It was a large clean place with plenty of room for many guests. About 50 people were invited and they all came. I hired a band—Johnny's favorite band. The invitation read that the party was to begin at 6PM and that everyone should come just a little before that time.

The band set up their instruments in a corner of the basement. I had ordered food and it was brought in at 6PM so that the guests could eat immediately. The band played as we all ate our meal. A large cake was brought in and my daughter

Joan quickly put the candles on it and lit them. The cake was placed in front of Johnny and he was asked to make a wish and then try to blow out the candles. The band played Happy Birthday while he blew and blew again and he got them all out. Everyone clapped. The band began to play one of our favorite songs and Johnny and I started dancing.

Everyone appeared to be enjoying themselves. The music was very good and most everyone got up to dance. It was a beautiful party and Johnny was honestly surprised and pleased. All the women kissed Johnny and wished him the very best. What will the next party be like?

Me and Johnny wearing one of the matching
outfits my mother made for us.

Jane surrounded by her family - Becky, Richie and Richard

Joan's Publicity Photo

Bud's hobby - collecting cars
Admiring his aquistion with his father

Nothing is better than breaking fresh baked bread with family and friends.

RYE BREAD
Ingredients:

2 cups potato water
2 tablespoons shortening
1 teaspoon caraway seed
1 cup butter milk
1/2 teaspoon ginger
3 to 4 cups white flour

1 cake yeast
3 tablespoons brown sugar
3 cups rye flour 1/4 cup warm water
1 tablespoon salt
1 tablespoon vinegar

Dissolve yeast in 1/4 cup warm water. Let stand a few minutes.
To the lukewarm potato water, add buttermilk, shortening, caraway seed, ginger, and vinegar.
Add the rye flour. Beat well. Add yeast and beat again.
Gradually add the rest of the white flour until the dough is stiff.
Turn out on floured board. Cover and let rest 10–15 minutes.
Then knead until smooth and blistered about 10 minutes.
Let rise in warm place until double in bulk. Punch down. Cover and let rise again.
Divide into three parts and let rest 10–12 minutes. Then shape into loaves.
Place in greased pans, cover, and let rise until light.
Place pans on center rack of 425 degree oven. Bake 25–30 minutes.
The pans should not touch each other or the sides of the oven.

38

In 1981, our daughter Jane had a baby boy. We became grandparents for the very first time. He was named Richard after his father, but everyone started calling him Richie and that's the name that stuck.

Two years later, Rebecca, who we called Becky, was born and now we had our first granddaughter. She was a cute baby and we were pleased that Richie now had a sister. Jane's family was growing which meant our family was growing. Everyone was so happy to have new titles like grandpa, grandma, aunt and uncle.

Jane is an exceptional mother. She always finds time to spend with her children. When they were small, she enjoyed walking around the block with them. She truly loves her children and they love her in return. Jane remembers how much time I spent with her as she was growing up and told me once that she wanted to be as good a mother as I was.

Joan had graduated from Northern Illinois University and was living in New York where she was pursuing a career in acting. She was always very busy in New York and often got parts in various venues such as plays, commercials and movies. None of the parts were major and she would eventually move to Los Angeles where she was able to get better parts on soap operas and in movies.

Bud had graduated from law school and was practicing near by. He had worked for another lawyer for a short time and then decided it was time he went out on his own. As he was just starting out, he didn't have money to pay a staff so I volunteered to help out in the office. So, I went there every day to answer the phones, open the mail and keep things organized. I loved the work and it was great to be able to go home at the end of the day and know that I was free until the following day.

It wasn't long before his business started to pick up and he plenty of referrals from clients who were happy with his service. I could say I was amazed at how fast his business grew, but knowing my son, it was no surprise at all.

We helped Bud buy a house and he got a dog that he dearly loved named, Sarge. Our son lived just a short distance from us so Johnny would drive over and let the dog out whenever we knew Bud would be late getting home.

Eventually, Bud felt it would be better for the dog to come to live at our house. We didn't mind because we felt it would be good for my mother-in-law,

Josephine, who was home a great deal of the time by herself as Johnny and I were always going someplace. Grandma Josephine learned to honestly love that dog as did Johnny and I. We felt she was safer at home with Sarge. He stayed by her side constantly to watch her and keep her feet warm as he slept on them.

My mother Helena and Johnny's mother Josephine
Still smiling and active after many birthdays.

My mother, Helena and Johnny's mother, Josephine both made excellent soups. Here's two of the family's favorites. There is nothing like a hot bowl of soup made with love to warm you inside and out.

HELENA'S CABBAGE SOUP
Ingredients:

2 to 3 lbs. of pork	1 Onion
1 Head of cabbage	Sour Cream
1 Carrot	

Place pork in pot and add water to cover. Bring to boil.
Remove scum from water.
Add cabbage, which has been cut up in small pieces.
Add carrot also cut up in small pieces.
Add onion cut up in small pieces.
Keep removing scum from top as it all boils.
After pork is soft, stop boiling.
Add sour cream before serving.

JOSEPHINE'S PEA SOUP
Ingredients:

1 to 2 pounds of chuck roast	½ cup of chopped onion
1 cup of dried green peas	Sour Cream to taste

Put 1 or 2 pounds of chuck meat into pot. Cover with water and boil.
Add mixture of 1 Cup dried green peas and ½ cup chopped onions.
Continue to boil until meat is soft.
Remove meat—add 1 or 2 T of sour cream and serve soup.

Cut meat into smaller pieces and serve on the side. Meat can be dipped in Ketchup, and eaten with rye bread. A nice salad goes well with this heartwarming meal.

39

Johnny's mother hadn't been feeling well nor eating very much. She would go into the den, sit in her favorite chair and watch television. I'd check on her regularly and within the hour I noticed she had fallen asleep. I turned off the TV and let her sleep. She slept for about an hour and then got up and walked into the kitchen. I asked her if she was hungry and she told me she wasn't. However, I quickly warmed up some soup and gave it to her. She slowly finished the soup and then wanted to return to the TV. Johnny walked her into the den and turned on the TV for her and gave her the remote control so she could change the channel if she wished. She sat there quietly for several hours while the night became dawn. The newspaper was brought in and Johnny took read it. I started to think about what I would make for breakfast and began to make preparations.

Later in the day, I walked into the den and I saw her sitting quietly in her chair as usual. The TV was on. I tried to talk to her but I don't know if she could hear me or was just too tired to converse. I called Johnny and told him to call the doctor. Johnny agreed with me. He thought we should know what we could to do to help her.

The doctor came and examined her. He told us it would be best if she were in the hospital where she would have 'round the clock' care. She didn't want to go but Johnny with the help of a neighbor got her into the car and we drove her to the hospital.

The nurse helped her get into bed and told her the doctor would be in shortly. I stayed with her. She had asked Johnny for her walker so she would be able to go to the washroom by herself. Johnny told her the walker was at home but he'd drive back there and pick it up for her. She put her head on the pillow and rested. Johnny left and I was alone with her. We talked for awhile and then she asked for her grandson. I told her he was at work but I would get in touch with him and I'm sure he'd come by as soon as he was able. I did call him and he was surprised grandma was in the hospital and promised he would be there shortly. I also got in touch with her granddaughters and they told me that they would come as soon as they were able to.

Then grandma turned her head, closed her eyes and I quickly called a nurse. She came and examined her and called several other nurses to come to help her.

They started to press down on her chest. She had a heart attack. I was asked to leave the room. I asked if I could stay with her but I was told that they needed to have all the room possible as they began to work on her.

I walked out into the hallway and began to cry. She really couldn't wait for all her grand children to reach the hospital. Within a short time a nurse came out of grandma's room and walked over to me and told me that they had done all they could for her, but couldn't save her. She died.

I cried, "Why couldn't you wait until all your grand children got to the hospital?" She couldn't because when you are called to go up to heaven you need to go immediately. She did. She is now watching us from there.

My husband arrived with the walker and saw me outside her room and asked why I wasn't in the room with ma. I told him I was until a short while ago when I was asked to leave and the nurses took over. I said to Johnny, "She left us for heaven just a short time ago." Johnny began to cry. Joan came into the room next and we all cried together.

Johnny loved his mother very much. She was always there to help him whenever he needed help or advice and now she wouldn't be there. "She'll be watching you from heaven. She'll try to advise you when she can," I comforted him.

Grandma Josephine was wheeled out of her room and taken downstairs to the morgue. We left for our house and started to make plans for the funeral. We all sat around the kitchen table and made plans as to what each would do. Bud was to call all her relatives and friends. Joan was to order the flowers—a casket spray and two end baskets. Johnny was to contact the speaker.

Oh, this was a very sad time for us all. Grandma would no longer be waiting for us when we came home. We all were going to miss her a great deal.

Finally, the funeral was set. There was music and then, Mr. Kostka, the speaker said a few words. Johnny also eulogized his mother. He spoke with deep sadness as he had just lost his dear mother.

After the service the friends and neighbors walked to their cars to prepare for a long hour ride to the cemetery. There, the speaker walked up to the casket and said a few words. There was a basket of flower petals on top of the casket. All were asked to take a few and drop them on top of the casket when it was lowered into the ground. We all cried as the petals fell to the casket. Grandma's body was now in the ground, but her soul was up in heaven. She's watching us from there now.

Using your noodle can mean more than cooking. I finally wised up and used my brains to learn how to drive at a very advanced age. And, I was good at it! Just as I was good at making this noodle dish.

KLUSKI KAPUSTA PO
(POLISH NOODLES AND CABBAGE)

Ingredients:

1/4 c Butter
1/2 c Yellow onion peeled, chopped
4 c Cabbage, chopped OR Thinly sliced
1 tsp Caraway seeds
1/2 tsp Salt
1/8 tsp Black pepper
8 oz Package of egg noodles
1/2 c Sour cream (optional)

Melt butter in a large skillet.
Add the onion and sauté until transparent.
Add the cabbage and sauté 5 minutes, or until tender but still crisp.
Stir in the caraway seeds, salt and pepper.

Meanwhile, cook the noodles in salted water as directed on package. Do not overcook. Drain well.

Stir the noodles into the cabbage and add the sour cream.
Cook five minutes longer, stirring frequently.

6 Servings

40

My husband and son loved to spend time together. One of the things they liked to do best was ride their motorcycles together. Johnny drove a Honda and Bud drove a Harley. They often took off with no destination in mind, just to go riding. But, every Sunday morning Bud would drive over to our house to pick up his dad and off they'd drive to the north side of Chicago to meet with several other motorcyclists to have breakfast. They enjoyed trading stories. This became a ritual that they looked forwarded to.

One day Johnny had an accident while out on the open road. He fell off the cycle and broke his leg. He was taken to the hospital where he remained for several weeks before he returned home to continue his journey of recovery. However, he couldn't do much due to his injuries, so he sat by the window and read a lot.

For 38 years, my husband had been my chauffer and drove me every place I needed to go. Now at age 68 I found we were unable to get around due to his accident. I had to rely on neighbors and friends to get us around. It was hard for me because I didn't know how to drive a car and so when we needed something from the store or if Johnny needed to go to the doctor, it was necessary to arrange for someone to take us and bring us home. There was a car in the garage, but I had no idea how to drive it. I was so frustrated because I wanted to take good care of my husband as he had always taken good care of me. So, I decided to take driving lessons.

I looked in the phone book for an instructor and found one nearby. I called him and told him what I wanted and asked if he was available. He said he would come to the house to pick me up within the next few days. When he came, he proceeded to explain everything in the car to me. Then he drove around the block and again explained everything he had done.

The following week he drove out to my house again, but this time he explained it would be best to get used to the car I would be driving. So, I opened up the garage door, got the keys to the car and he backed it out of the garage. He started by letting me drive around the block where there was hardly any traffic.

After several sessions of doing this he decided I was ready for traffic. I drove to the entrance of our subdivision and made a left hand turn onto Meyers Road and headed for 22nd Street. Both streets are very busy and now I had to make another left hand turn onto 22nd Street. The instructor was very calm and patient and talked to me throughout the whole thing. I drove a short distance and then came upon some men who were doing repair work on the street. Again the instructor sat at my side and explained how to proceed. I did, but I was scared the whole time.

We then approached an intersection and the light was red so I stopped. He instructed me to make a right had turn on Highland Ave., another busy street. We stayed on Highland until 31st Street where I turned again. This was all very hard for me and I was afraid, but I was determined to learn how to drive.

When I finally reached my house, my instructor told me that I did fine, but I needed more practice. I felt very happy that I had driven on 22nd Street. While it was a busy street, it felt like I was really driving for the first time. Now I was anxious to master driving so I wouldn't need to depend on the neighbors to take me to the store.

I was very lucky to have such a good instructor who took the time to explain everything to me and had the patience to teach me to drive. After a month of taking lessons, I thought I would go to the Driver's License station and apply for a license. I did and was given a test and passed. I was so happy. Now I could easily drive my husband to his doctor and hospital appointments.

When the driving instructor came the next day I told him what I did. He was happy for me, but told me I really need a little more practice. I honestly understood that I did need more practice and he continued to come to my house for the next month. We would drive together and I would learn more and more, but the best part was the confidence I gained during this time. I was beginning to feel comfortable behind the wheel.

I was also getting practice on my own. I would take Johnny in the car with me and he would give me directions on how to get where we needed to go. Johnny became my teacher now and would continually guide me. I listened carefully to him and we always got to where we needed to go.

Finally, it was time to end the lessons. My instructor was happy for me, but disappointed for himself as he would no longer be receiving my fees for his lesson. I never saw him again after that, but I am eternally grateful that I have the independence to now drive myself.

Our dog Sarge loved to sit in the driver's seat.
If a dog can drive, so can I!

Me leading the band in Czechoslovakia
after winning a contest

Traveling to different towns and different countries can be just ducky!

DUCK GIBLETS AND RICE
Ingredients:

Duck giblets
Water
2 Cups of Rice (or more depending on how much water is used)
2 tbsp butter
I chopped onion

In a hot pot put the butter and the chopped onion until it gets soft and tender. Add the washed giblets, which have been removed from the duck and place in a large pot. Cover with water, add salt, and cook on stove until the water boils.
Continue cooking for about 45 minutes to an hour.
When the meat is getting soft, remove it from the pot and cut it up into very small pieces.
The pieces should be soft. If not, return to water and boil some more.

Once all the meat is cooked and removed from the water, boil the rice in this water that has just been seasoned by the meat.

Boil until rice is soft and ready to eat.

Mix the meat pieces in with the rice.

Salt and pepper generously.

Wahlaa! A delicious meal!!

41

When my husband was strong and healthy enough to be left home alone I decided to help my son Bud with his law practice. He had rented an office nearby in Lombard and I helped him arrange it. Once he was all settled, I worked on a daily basis answering the phone when he was out or busy. I was there when the mail arrived and I opened it and had it ready for my son to handle. If there was something I could handle, I would.

I did all I could to help him and he was doing rather well. He soon felt he needed to move because his clients couldn't always find him where his office was located. His office was the last one in a cluster of offices and not easy to see. He started looking around and found an office to his liking not far away from this office and told his current landlord he was moving.

The following weekend he asked several of his good buddies to help him move. They did and now he was located in a small building near the center of town. He advertised in the local papers and had a huge sign made up for the outside of the building. Now people could easily find his office and he was happy.

He was getting quite a few customers and he handled them all well. This increased his business tremendously as his clients would tell their friends who would then come to him for help too.

It had been 14 years since we went to Europe with my brother Lou and we decided it was time to go again, so in 1989 we book a tour to see 10 countries and 9 capitals in Europe. One of the highlights of this trip was our visit to the Berlin Wall. It had already been in the process of coming down. I believe someone was anxious to get it down and started the process. There was a man working on the wall and when he chopped out a small brick he would hold it up in the air and ask if anyone wanted to buy it. If someone bought it, he would start chipping away at the wall to loosen another piece of brick.

No other person was allowed to go near the wall. He was the only one allowed to break down the wall or remove the bricks. Once he had a piece of brick he would wash it and rinse it before selling it. Many wanted these small tokens of history for souvenirs. I believe he made a nice piece of change doing this.

After Germany, we visited Switzerland. I loved the snow capped mountains and was thrilled when the bus driver agreed to stop the bus and let us get off near a Swiss glacier. Johnny and I quickly hopped off the bus and had one of our friends take a picture of us throwing snowballs at each other. As everyone started to get on the bus, I spied a bear in the distance. I couldn't believe I was actually looking at a big bear in the Alps. I decided to get a little closer and try to get a picture of the bear to show friends back home. Slowly and quietly I started to advance on the bear, which really looked very sweet from a distance. All of a sudden, the bear noted my approach, growled and started heading my way. I started to run for the bus and when I reached the door I began pounding against it for the driver to open up. He didn't and the bear was getting closer. I ran to the other end of the bus to try to hide from the bear, but the bear was not fooled. I continued to run around the bus until I got back to the door and pounded again on the door. Finally, the bus driver opened it. I looked at him angrily and asked, "Why didn't you open the door when I pounded." He drolly replied, "I never let anyone with a 'bare' behind in the bus."

We went on to Czechoslovakia which was the highlight of the tour for my husband. This is the country of his grandparents' birth and to him it was going home. One night while we were there, we decided to go dancing. We asked for directions to a place that would have a band playing and where we could dance. There was a night club not far from our hotel and we went. We were the only Americans in the audience, but my husband speaks the language fluently and could translate anything for me. So, when they had an audience participation contest I joined in. I was so surprised when I won and found that the prize was leading the band for their next song. I had never done anything like this before, but I had the time of my life waving the baton and keeping them in time.

One of the reasons we selected this particular tour was because we would be in a position to visit my mother's hometown in Poland. We drove to the border of Poland, but we were no allowed to enter. There was a policeman there and he turned us back on the road. I so wanted to see where she lived and what the area was like. My hope at the time was that things would change and when I returned to Europe the next time I would be able to finally visit my ancestral village.

Me and Johnny dancing at our
40th Wedding Anniversary Party

These two breads were always a hit with the crowd when baked goods were called for at a meeting. Both recipes became famous in the seventies, but still are popular today.

ZUCCHINI BREAD
Ingredients:

2 Cup Sugar	1 Cup Shortening
3 Eggs	2 tsp. Vanilla
3 Cups Flour	1 tsp. Salt
1 Cup Nuts (chopped)	3 tsp. Baking Soda
¼ tsp. Baking Powder	2 tsp. Cinnamon
2 Cups Zucchini (pureed in blender or grated)	

Combine sugar, shortening, eggs and vanilla until well mixed.
Sift together flour, baking soda, baking powder, salt and cinnamon.
Add to above mixture.
Add zucchini and mix well.

Bake at 350 degrees in bread pan for 1 hour.
Makes two loafs.

BANANA NUT LOAF
Ingredients:

½ Cup Butter	2 Cups sifted Flour
1 Cup Sugar	½ tsp. Salt
2 Eggs	3 tsp. Baking Powder
1 Cup mashed Bananas	1 Cup chopped Nuts
1 tsp. Lemon Juice	

Mix butter and sugar until creamy.
Beat eggs until light and add to butter mixture.
Mash bananas and add lemon juice. Blend with creamed mixture and add flour mixture.
Add chopped nuts.
Bake in greased loaf pan at 375 degrees for 1 hr 15 min.

42

My husband and I have always been game for a party and have thrown many parties over the years. When we were approaching our 40th Wedding Anniversary, we decided to have a big party to celebrate. We wanted to show our friends how much we still loved each other and how happy our marriage has been.

We started by deciding where to hold the party and then composing our guest list. Once we knew how many people would be coming, we called the hall to make sure they could accommodate 300 guests and when they said they could, we booked the room. The following day we visited the place and picked up a sample menu from which to choose what we would like to serve at the dinner. Once we established the menu, we decided on a time for our guests to arrive and depart that was in line with how many hours we would have the room. Then Johnny called his good friend Rudy Drnek to see if his band would be able to play at our party. They were available and we were so pleased that everything was coming together as planned.

Johnny and I went to the printer and picked out cards and had all the necessary information for the invitations to our party. At this point, it seemed like we were doing all the things we didn't do when we had gotten married forty years ago. It was all so much fun and we felt like kids again.

Once the invitations arrived, we started to address all the envelopes and get them ready to mail. This was an enormous job as each invitation also included an RSVP card. We tackled the job and got them all off to the post office. But, there was still so much to do. I needed a new dress and Johnny wanted a new suit for the party. We wanted to be sure that our outfits went well together so I had to buy my dress first.

Finally, all the details were taken care of and the day of the party arrived. It was a beautiful day, which was in our favor. People wouldn't have a difficult time driving to the banquet hall. Johnny and I arrived at the hall a half an hour before the party was to begin. We checked the tables and had a list as to where each guest would be seated. The band arrived and set up their music and instruments. Everything was coming along nicely. The head waitress checked with us as to when we wanted the meal served and verified the menu.

Johnny and I greeted each guest as they arrived. Soon, there was festivity in the air and the room began to fill up with our family and friends. As people found their places at the table, we continued to make the rounds and spending a little more time with each person. Their good wishes and kisses were overflowing and we felt so lucky to have such good friends.

The waitresses started to serve the food and it all smelled so good and looked so beautiful on the platters. Just as we were about to begin, our son Bud rose and proposed a toast to us. He was eloquent to the point that he was reciting French proverbs and we were so pleased with his words.

Once dinner was over, my husband gave a speech thanking everyone for helping us celebrate our anniversary. He felt he should tell the guests about our wedding since precious few of them had been there. He also caught them up with what he have been doing since his retirement.

All of our children were there as well as our two grandchildren we had at the time. We danced to music of Rudy Drnek's band and he played special songs for us. My favorite was the old standard, *"Alley Cat."* For Johnny they played, *"Oh, Johnny."* Of course, Johnny and I had the dance floor to ourselves for the first dance, but then our friends began to surround us dancing as if they were still in their teens. All in all, it was a great day.

John Jr. and Lourdes on their Wedding Day
Our son always surprised us as he did this
day arriving in a helicopter

I always thought of stuffed peppers as a special meal. We didn't make it often, but when we did, it was for a special occasion. And, special occasions are what we live for—aren't they?

STUFFED GREEN PEPPERS
Ingredients:

6 medium green peppers
1 1/2 lbs ground beef
1 cup cooked rice
1/2 cup chopped onions
1/2 cup chopped celery
1 cup diced tomato
1 teaspoon minced garlic
1 teaspoon salt
1/2 teaspoon pepper
1 (10 ounce) can tomato soup
1/2 teaspoon basil

Cut tops off peppers, remove seeds.
Drop in boiling water for 3 minutes.
Drain, rinse in cold water
In a bowl, combine the next 8 ingredients.
Spoon into peppers.
Put in a greased 13x9in pan.
Mix soup and basil.
Spoon over peppers.
Cover and bake at 350° for 1 hour.

(6 servings)

43

Our son traveled extensively as he was studying international law. He had many friends around the world that he had met when they visited in the United States and they always asked him to visit them when he was in their country. Even if Bud had no one to travel with, this did not stop him—he went anyway.

One time when he was traveling in South America, he met a bright and spirited woman named Lourdes. He immediately fell in love with her. He had such a big personality himself and was so gregarious that he had always wanted a woman who was strong in her own right. When he found that their feelings of love were mutual, he went to her father to get his approval for marriage.

Soon afterward, Lourdes, who we fondly call Luli, came to the United States and married my son in a ceremony that took place at the Pacific Club—a restaurant near our home. The place was closed to everyone except those invited to the wedding. Even though the notice was very short, many people attended the wedding including our daughter Joan who flew in from California.

When everyone was gathered and waiting for the ceremony to begin, we began to get nervous because no one knew where Bud was. Suddenly, there was a commotion and everyone went rushing to the front of the building just in time to see Bud arriving in a helicopter he had rented for the occasion. He had a flamboyant nature and what better day to show off than on your wedding day?

The entire event was an overwhelming success with Bud and Luli leaving on their honeymoon by helicopter after all the festivities were completed. We had eaten, danced, visited and celebrated.

Several of our friends belonged to the West Suburban Dance Club and we were asked to join the club. The club met at a different ballroom each month to dance away the evening. Before each dance, a club member prepared hors douerves and invited everyone to their house to enjoy a social hour. We enjoyed this group very much and soon we were dancing every week! Anytime a few members wanted to get together and meet at a ballroom or dance, we would go.

The more we got to know the club members, the more we were happy to belong to it. As time went on many members found it rather difficult to have club members come to their house. Therefore we took a vote as to whether or not to continue this or else find a place to serve coffee and bakery goods before dancing.

We asked the place where we were dancing if we could bring in food and coffee for a social time before dancing and they agreed. Now, each month two couples got together and decided what would be served. Sometimes we would have hors doeurves, coffee and bakery and other times just bakery items and coffee. This was easier for all. After the refreshments, the band began to play and we began to dance.

We all got along beautifully. However, since I've gotten ill, we no longer belong to this group. I can't dance any longer, however, when I get well again, I'll check with some of the members as to whether or not we could join again.

There is nothing Bohemian or Polish about veal and spinach...it's just good food for hungry people.

SESAME VEAL CUTLETS
Ingredients:

1 Egg	2 tbsp. Sesame Seeds
2 tsp. Lemon Juice	½ Cup Bread Crumbs
2 tsp. Lemon Rind	¼ Cup Flour
1 tsp. Salt	Veal Cutlets
Pepper	

Combine egg, juice, rind, salt and pepper. Mix well.
Mix sesame seeds with bread crumbs.
Dredge cutlets in flour, then egg mixture, then bread crumbs.
Refrigerate for ½ hour.
Cook over medium heat until done.

SPINACH
Ingredients:

Spinach
Salt
Butter
Onion (chopped into small pieces)
Garlic (chopped into small pieces)
Flour
Hard boiled egg (crumbled)

Boil spinach in salted water.
In a frying pan, melt a small amount of butter, add onions and garlic and cook for a few minutes.
Add flour and cook until brown.
When spinach is done, drain and cut into small pieces.
Put into pan and quickly fry with onion and butter mixture.
Remove from heat and garnish with crumbled egg.

44

One of my fondest memories took place in 1992. Our son had gotten tickets to see Bill Clinton be inaugurated as president of the United States. At the time, our son Bud owned an office building in Batavia, Illinois. Republican congressman Bill Hassert rented office space from Bud. Bud, who had his law offices in the building, and Bill would visit each other's office when time permitted and they became good friends. After Bud got the tickets, he found that he was unable to go. He asked us if we wanted to go in his place. Johnny and I immediately said, "Yes!" He made air and hotel reservations for us and with tickets in hand, we were ready to go.

We took the plane and arrived in Washington D.C. on a beautiful day. We were so fortunate to have a hotel with such a good location. In the evening we were able to watch everything from our hotel window. The fireworks were awe inspiring. There was a huge crowd below all waiting for the President to arrive. We waited too, but we sat in the comfortable chairs in our room as we waited.

The following day, we decided we'd go to tour the White House. There were many who had the same idea so there was a long line of people waiting to be admitted. We got in line too and we were very lucky because our line was chosen to go inside rather quickly.

We walked up the stairs to the front door and we were ushered inside. After a short tour, we were asked to line up in order to see the President and Vice President. We were practically in the front of the line and were able to wish them both the best. I actually kissed President Bill Clinton and Vice President Al Gore. I just kissed them on the cheek though.

At the actual inauguration, we stood near the stage and had a great view of the ceremony. The President was tall and handsome. It was inspiring to be there and hear the President utter the solemn words that that make us feel secure and proud to be American. There was a large parade afterwards. The president walked with his wife to their new home—the White House.

At the time of the inauguration, Bud was very busy getting established with his law practice, buying property, building a house and nourishing his marriage. It was only a few years later, in 1995 that Bud and Luli had a daughter who they named after Johnny's mother—Josephine. We were so delighted to welcome this cherished child into our family and practically begged for them to let us baby sit her.

When they did have functions to attend or just needed time together, they would let Josephine come over and we would have a wonderful time. She was an easy going baby and more lovable than you can imagine. I enjoyed my time with her. We played games together. Grandpa would play the piano and we would sing along. When she got a little older, he began to show her how to play simple songs and he delighted in this.

I loved bathing her and getting her ready for bed at night. It would take me back to the days when my children were young. Before I would put her to bed, I would tell her stories about my own childhood and she was always very attentive. Then Grandpa would also tell a story and then we would tuck her in, kiss her and put out the lights.

When the weather was warm, we'd take her to the playground and she enjoyed that very much. She'd slide down the slide, swing on the swings and when she was very young, she loved playing in the sandbox. No matter what she was doing on the playground, I was always nearby. I didn't want her to get hurt in any way.

Whenever we were out of the house and a mealtime was here, we'd take Josephine to eat at a nearby restaurant. She was always so excited to be eating out, she behaved perfectly. Of course, when her parents came to pick her up we were always sad to see her go and looked forward immediately to the next time we would be able to baby sit again.

I also seemed so busy and rushed when my children were small that I never really paused to enjoy the necessary duties of motherhood. With Josephine, I could and it meant a lot to me.

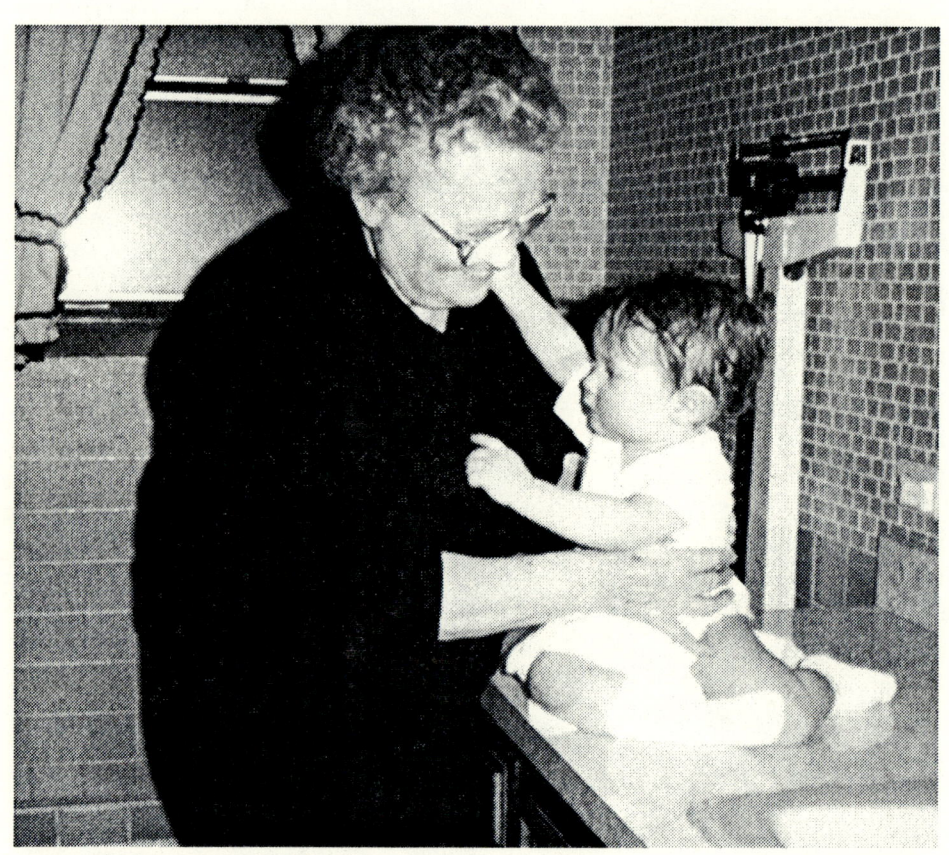

Me with my grandaughter, Josephine, who has just had a refreshing bath.

When the soul reaches its darkest hour and you still need sustenance, there is nothing like comfort food.

CHICKEN PAPRIKASH
Ingredients:

1 chicken (3–4 lbs.)
1 medium onion, chopped
¼ c. butter
½ tsp. paprika
1-½ cup water
½ c sour cream
2 tbs. flour

Cut chicken into small pieces.
Wilt onion in butter, add paprika, chicken and salt; brown.
Add water, cover and simmer until tender (about 45 min.).
Remove chicken from pan.
Mix sour cream with flour, stir carefully into pan, simmer gravy for five minutes strain over chicken.

(note: in place of butter, chopped bacon can be used to brown the onion in.)

45

Our son Bud became very ill. When he went to the doctor for a checkup, tests were ordered that determined he had cancer. Immediately, he was sent to the hospital for surgery and part of his stomach was removed. After the surgery, he returned to work, but we could tell that he was still sick.

Bud became interested in Christian Science. It may have been too late for medicine to heal him, so he looked for spiritual help in healing through this organization. While they advise all members to seek medical help based on their own consciousness, Bud decided to put his full faith in the church. He no longer went to see his doctor.

But, alas, he continued to decline in health. His wife, Luli, brought him over to our house one weekend to stay with us. She had been taking care of him day and night for months, and exhausted, she felt she needed a break. He was in a wheelchair as his body was too weak to support his large frame. I loved taking care of him and spending time with him, but I was also taking care of my husband who was recovering from his fall down a flight of stairs. It was all too much for me.

The next week, I was in Bud's office when an ambulance driver came into Bud's office and told Bud that he should go to the ambulance outside and they'll drive him to the hospital. "Who ordered the ambulance?" Bud was very upset that he'd be going to the hospital. "Who ordered the ambulance?" How could this happen? I left the office, locked the doors and started to drive to my house. When I arrived at home, I told my husband about what had happened. I lied down on my bed. I was very upset.

My husband and I drove to the hospital and asked as to what his room number was. We were told he was in intensive care. We went up to that room and found him lying in bed. Oh, I became frightened.

The following day I was babysitting Josephine at our home. We were pulling weeds outside when suddenly I fell to the ground unconscious. Blood was coming out of my ear. Josephine ran to get Grandpa. They called the ambulance. I heard that Josephine tried to put a band-aid over my ear to help me. I had suffered a devastating stroke that would change my life forever. I was placed on the 5th floor stroke unit of the hospital and Bud was on the 4th floor cardiac care unit.

My husband was still in considerable pain and not very mobile so it was difficult for him to come to the hospital. He could not drive because of his accident. He could hardly even walk. Joan drove him daily to the hospital to see Bud and I. Bud and his friend, Greg Carnduf, came to visit me in rehab. Greg wheeled Bud into my room. I was so glad to see him, but I could barely speak to him because of my stroke. I could hardly look at him too because my head would only turn to the right. I could not get out of bed. He seemed to be doing better than I was. I sure did hope he was.

Joan spent every night with me while I was in a coma. The nurses let her sleep at my bedside. She held my hand and massaged it day and night for several days until I regained consciousness. Then she fed me and let the nurses have some time off. Joan is still friends with the nurses who attended to me then.

Weeks later, I was doing better and was able to come home. Bud was back at his home by then too, but not for long. Soon he was back in intensive care. Even though I could barely walk I wanted to see him very badly, so Joan drove us to the hospital every day for the many weeks he was in intensive care. She wheeled us each to his room every night. I was in such poor condition that I could not stay long at these visits. My heart truly broke to see my son suffering. I could not hide my tears whenever I saw him. It was very difficult for me, but I know it was even more difficult for Bud.

He lived for many weeks on life support in intensive care. On November 13, 1998, he was taken off of life support. I so hoped he would breathe on his own and get his strength back. He died within an hour of being off life support. When he died, I was at his bedside with Bud's wife, Luli, and his best friend, Rick Stvan. I picked up his hand and kissed it. I stayed next to his bed just looking at him. There were so many machines there that he had been hooked up to. Everything that happened remains a blur to me. A nurse came in to check Bud and told us that he had died. His doctor was standing in the doorway and I asked him to please check Bud as I could not believe that he was dead. The doctor walked over to the bed, checked him and nodded that he was gone. I felt terrible. I never got a chance to talk to him. Johnny and Joan came into the room shortly after he had taken his last breath. We all held hands and made a circle around his bed. We all cried. In a short time, the nurses came into the room and disconnected the machines that were hooked up to his body. The following hours were terrible. We were told to leave our son and since there was nothing we could do, we decided to leave. He was taken out of the room and down the hall. We lingered in the hallway a long time, watching, crying, in shock over everything. To this day, I still have not recuperated enough from my stroke to fully process my son's death. It was the saddest day of my life. Sometimes I feel like it just happened and I still cry often over my son's death.

The following day we went to the Westchester Funeral Home to begin making arrangements. His daughter was just 3 years old then and she adored her Auntie Joan. Joan played with Josephine in the chapel so that we could make the arrangements and so that Josephine could be a child on this difficult day. It must have been very difficult for Joan to be taking care of all of us when she too was grieving her only brother's death. She was our strong support when we were all falling apart. She also became a special part of Josephine's life and helped Johnny and I to see Josephine every Friday. Joan would pick her up from school and we would go out for ice cream and have dinner together. It meant so much for us to continue to be in Josephine's life. She looked so much like Bud and she had his gregarious personality too. She is so quickly growing up into a very beautiful young lady.

Since I've had my stroke, I am not able to do all I did before. I can no longer drive my car. I get tired very easily and lie down many times during the day. I feel tired and am unable to do many of the things I did before the stroke.

When I think of my son, I feel a tear in my eye. Oh Bud why did you leave us so soon? You had just finished building your new office building and honestly didn't get a chance to use it. Can you see me from heaven? We miss you and think of you very much. We go out often to your new house in the ground. Hope you're comfortable there and I must tell you that you looked very handsome as you lied in the casket. Bud, I imagine you've met some of your friends who have left earth as you did. Josephine is getting older and she misses you. When she's at our house, she'll mention you to us many times. Watch over her.

We have many wonderful memories of you in our hearts. I truly remember the day that you were born. I carried you in my arms out of our room to where Dad was and told him, "Johnny, Johnny, it's a boy—just as you wanted." Dad was very happy to have a son and now you've left us. However, please watch over us, if possible. You're constantly on our minds.

Joan drove dad and me to the cemetery today to see your grave. We bought some flowers and placed them on your grave. There was a poinsettia plant on the grave. I imagine Luli or Josephine placed it there. Oh Bud, I sure do miss you. I have more time at home since I don't drive to the office as I did when you were there.

John A. Budilovsky, Jr.

1952 - 1998
B.S., M.B.A., J.D., LL.M.

From John's Chicago Tribune Obituary: John A. Budilovsky, 46, a Batavia lawyer and active community leader, died Friday in Hinsdale Hospital. A native of Chicago, Mr. Budilovsky graduated from Provise West High School. He later graduated from Kent College of Law and obtained degrees in international law, taxation, and marketing from universities throughout the world. Mr. Budilovsky traveled the world, meeting his wife, Lourdes, in Peru. During his varied career, he was a college marketing professor, a car salesman, a real estate developer, and a lawyer. Mr. Budilovsky moved to Batavia in the early 1990's and immersed himself in the community. He helped to rebuild the business district when he purchased an 84-year-old building and renovated it for his law offices. He received numerous architectural awards for his efforts. A collector of antique motorcylces and cars, Mr. Budilovsky showcased his fleet every year during the annual Batavia parade. Survivors include his wife, Lourdes "Luli;" a daughter, Josephine; his parents, John and Leona; and two sisters, Jane Zeck and Joan.

Home isn't always a physical address. It is where you find the people you love, the smell of good food and your own bed to sleep in.

KASHA
This is a European dish.

Ingredients:

5 to 10 potatoes (You usually need at least 2 potatoes per individual).
Salt and Pepper to taste
Eggs
Bacon (optional)

Peel potatoes, wash them and then grate them into large bowl. (You can also use a food processor, but you will need to add a bit of water.) As potatoes are grated, place in a colander lined with cheese cloth. Be sure to have the colander in the sink or over bowl as potatoes will start to sweat. Add about a teaspoon or so of salt (depending on how many potatoes you use) and stir. Taking up the ends of the cheese cloth, create a bundle and squeeze any moisture out of the potatoes.
Beat eggs until yolk and whites are mixed and coat grated potatoes. (Use a ratio of 1 egg to 5 potatoes)
Put mixture into a baking dish
Lay three strips of bacon across the top of the potatoes. (optional)
As the kasha bakes, the potatoes will become thicker and sticky. It is recommended that you use a Teflon baking pan or that you grease and flour the pan before use.
Bake at 300 to 350 degrees until sides start turning brown. Check frequently and stir if necessary. A large batch will take about three hours to bake.

46

Oh, time changes everything. We both still love to dance however we're not as able as we once were.

John and I celebrated our 50 years of marriage together in the year 2000! We had a party at a reception hall called Alesandro's. Three hundred people were present. We were served a delicious dinner and then the music started. Our favorite band was hired. Everyone was pleased with our choice of music. Most of our friends were about our age therefore, we knew how much they enjoyed the music as well. We had professional ballroom dancers come to entertain us too. What a beautiful performance they gave. The women's dresses were elegant and flowed with their graceful movements as the men in their handsome tuxes twirled them around the dance floor. Many of our friends can no longer dance, so we were all able to enjoy the glorious movements of these fine dancers.

As much as we loved being able to celebrate our 50th anniversary, we were sad that our son who had always toasted us at past parties was not there. Of course, our daughters Joan and Jane were present and they really made the affair festive. So many people were gone now. My mother and father were both gone as well as Johnny's parents. While our family members who have gone were not there physically, I knew that they were with us nonetheless.

I could remember how I was able to go around and greet everyone at my 40th anniversary and oh how I danced. While this anniversary party was every bit as memorable, neither Johnny nor I danced and the guests came to the head table to greet us this time. Johnny was still not up to snuff after having fallen down a flight of stairs and I was still recovering from my stroke at the time—even though it had been two years. I am so glad that we have the party to look back on and remember and hope that when our 60th anniversary comes along that we will have a party just as good.

Over 300 guests came to our 50th Anniversary Party. Beautiful ballroom dancers entertained us all and made the celebration even more magical!

When you need something easy but impressive, this is the recipe for you.

FRUIT COFFEE CAKE
Ingredients:

½ Cup Butter
1 Cup Sugar
2 Cups Flour
2 tsp. Baking Powder

½ tsp. Salt
½ Cup Milk
2 Eggs (beaten)
Fruit

Mix: Butter, Sugar, Flour, Baking Powder and Salt till a coarse crumb mixture forms.
Reserve: 1 Cup
Add to Remaining Mixture: Milk and Eggs—Mix Well
Pour into greased 9" X 13" pan.
Cover mixture with your favorite fruit
Sprinkle the reserved mixture on top so that all the fruit is covered
Sprinkle a little sugar over top
Bake at 350 degrees for about 25 minutes.

47

My granddaughter Becky, who was in high school, was studying about Europe and wanted to see what it was like. Perhaps it was as she was told or maybe it was different. She had studied about Germany under the reign of Hitler and his Nazi's. I also wanted to return to Europe because on both previous occasions I was unable to see the town of my mother's birth in Vilnius. Vilnius is now in Lithuania, but back then, it was considered to be in Poland. I hoped that another visit would allow me to see her old home and the places she talked about as I was growing up.

I spoke to my husband of my desire to go back to Europe. He thought it was a great idea, but he did not feel that he was well enough to go. He still encouraged me to go though, so I offered to treat Joan and my granddaughter Becky on this European trip. They were thrilled to join me and I was thrilled for them to come! Joan and I quickly got busy planning the details of our trip. What great fun we had doing this too!

Our first stop was Vilnius. We were able to visit many historic places, including St. Helena's Cathedral, but we were still not able to locate my mother Helena's home. We tried very hard though. We spent hours digging into historical archives in the old government buildings there to try and find the exact location. Although we never found the house, being with my children in this lovely city amidst all our treasured ancestry was a great joy indeed. I remember one cold night in particular. We had been hunting in the government archives all day and decided to treat ourselves to a cup of hot chocolate at a small café. It was the best hot chocolate I ever had. It was like drinking pure melted Hershey bars. Yum! Vilnius was filled with special treasures—old outdoor markets, delicious ethnic food, and an array of kind people. We even met up with one of Becky's friends who was serving there in Mormon missionary service. Vilnius is a special place. We loved our time there.

From Vilnius, we took a train to Krakow, Poland. What a marvelous time we had enjoying this artistic city. It is the home town of the current pope and the people who live there are certainly proud of this important fact. There was happy music playing in the streets and artists selling their special wares everywhere. Becky, Joan and I, bought matching handmade sweaters in the large outdoor market outside our hotel. The nights were cold and we needed these extra sweaters to keep us warm. Despite the cold, Joan found this magical city of Krakow her most favorite city of all. Little did she know then that her future husband's grandparents would be from Krakow. Magical indeed!

After Krakow, we traveled by train to Prague, Czechoslovakia. Prague is much bigger than Krakow, and more majestic in its beauty. We stayed at a lovely small hotel in the center of Old Town. We enjoyed the cobblestone streets and all the incredible history there. We even went to the opera one night where Mozart had performed hundreds of years earlier. One day we traveled outside Prague to the small city of Blovice, to see where Johnny's relatives, our children's paternal ancestry came from. It was a small city, a few hours outside of Prague. We hired a car service to drive us there. It was beautiful to drive through the Czech countryside to this lovely quaint town of Blovice. We looked up, "Budilovsky" in the phone book there and actually found some relatives to meet. They greeted us into their homes and made us feel so welcomed. We will forever remember their kind hospitality.

I was so pleased to be able to take Joan and Becky on this trip and make history come alive. I am sure that as memorable as the trip was for me, it was also for them. It was truly an incredible time. We all want to go again!

Modeling our new matching sweaters in the lobby of the Hotel Rezydent in Krakow, Poland

Here we are outside St. Helena's Church in Vilnius, Lithuania

Booksigning tours take a lot of energy. There is nothing that can boost you up better than liver. It goes nicely with a warm hearty dressing to fill you up.

DRESSING
Ingredients:

2 tbsp. Margarine	1 Onion
2 Cloves of Garlic	½ lb. Crackers
3 Eggs	Cup Milk

In frying pan melt margarine. Add chopped onion and minced garlic.
Cook until onion is transparent.
Mix together crushed crackers, eggs and milk. Add onion mix.
Place in baking pan.
Bake at 350 degrees for one hour.

LIVER AND ONIONS
Ingredients:

Beef Liver	Bacon
Onions	Salt
Pepper	Flour

Fry bacon, when rather crisp, remove from frying pan and crumble.
Fry chopped onion in fat from bacon, remove from pan.
Place liver in fat—add salt, pepper and a light dusting of flour.
Fry for about 8 minutes on each side.
Put onion and bacon back in pan and warm. Serve

48

Joan is very creative and she is very good at making our life interesting. For my husband's 87th birthday, Joan suggested we go to Michigan and visit the Ford Museum. Johnny has had a lifelong love affair with cars and he always wanted to go to the museum, but we never made the time. Joan made all the arrangements. She bought train tickets from Chicago to Detroit, made hotel reservations and rented a car. We left for Michigan the day before Johnny's birthday.

We visited the Ford Museum on Johnny's birthday. We entered the museum and he began to look at everything. He didn't want to miss a thing. It was wonderful to see him so happy. Neither Johnny nor I can walk long distances, but Joan took care of everything making sure we had wheelchairs and that we didn't miss even one exhibit. I couldn't think of a more fitting birthday present for my husband.

After a full day of experiencing the museum, Joan took us out for dinner and then back to our hotel. The next day we went to visit our friends in Lansing, Michigan. Karen Martin and Jeff Hibbs have two adorable little boys, McKee and Cierdon. These two little guys really kept us hopping! Later that day, Joan and I spoke at a booksigning event at a popular Lansing, Bookstore. It was right in the middle of a college town and was all great fun. It was exciting to see my book, *My Mother, Helena,* featured in newspapers and posters all around Michigan…right along with Joan's many books! Little did I know then, this would be the beginning of many more mother-daughter booksigning events. It has been wonderful sharing these exciting events with family and friends.

BORDERS®
My Mother Helena
Leona Turlo Budilovsky
Yoga
Massage
Meditation
Join us at Borders this month for a very special
MOTHER-DAUGHTER
booksigning event!
Join Joan and Leona Turlo Budilovsky for a very special mother-daughter booksigning! Leona Turlo Budilovsky will be signing copies of her memoir, MY MOTHER, HELENA. Her book is the inspiring true story of her mother Helena Turlo's courage in the face of war-torn Poland during World War I. Through the loss of family, friends, and a cherished European way of life, she is forced to begin again in Chicago. Leona's daughter Joan, a yoga instructor, meditation teacher, and certified massage therapist, will be signing copies of her books, "THE COMPLETE IDIOT'S GUIDE TO YOGA, THE COMPLETE IDIOT'S GUIDE TO MEDITATION, and THE COMPLETE IDIOT'S GUIDE TO MASSAGE. Joan will be discussing all three subjects: disciplines that can help us all achieve health and balance in our lives.
A BOOK DISCUSSION AND SIGNING WITH AUTHORS
JOAN & LEONA TURLO
BUDILOVSKY
SUNDAY, JUNE 22ND AT 4:00PM
BORDERS BOOKS AND MUSIC IN NORRIDGE
7100 FOREST PRESERVE DRIVE
CALL (708) 457-2111 FOR MORE INFORMATION

Joan and Ben on their Wedding Day
February 14, 2004

The happiness of our children has always been paramount in our life. To see contentment and love in the eyes of your child is the best present in the world and cause to celebrate...and these cookies are great for parties.

CHEESE CAKE COOKIES
Ingredients for crust:

2/3 Cup Brown Sugar
2/3 Cup Butter (softened)
2 Cups Flour
1 Cup Walnuts (chopped)

Cream butter and sugar until fluffy.
Add flour and nuts and mix until crumbly.
Reserve 1 cup of mixture.
Press remaining mixture into the bottom of 9" X 13" pan
Bake at 350 degrees for 12 to 15 minutes.

Ingredients for filling:

¾ Cup Sugar
3–8 oz. packages of Cream Cheese
3 Eggs
6 tbsp. Milk
1 ½ tbsp. Vanilla
3 tbsp. Lemon Juice

Blend sugar and cream cheese until smooth.
Add eggs, milk vanilla and lemon juice. Beat well.
Spread over baked crust.
Sprinkle reserved crust mixture over top.
Bake at 350 degrees for 45 minutes.
Cool, cut and refrigerate.

49

We still have surprises and delights in our life. Recently our family increased in size when our daughter Joan married the man of her dreams, Ben Kuzniar. We liked him from the minute we met him and knew that he would make our daughter very happy.

On Valentine's day, February 14, 2004, Joan and Ben were married at Porticuncula Chapel located at the Peabody Estate not far from our home in Oakbrook. She had decided she wanted an intimate wedding with only family members and the closest of friends present.

My husband and I were excited as Joan took us shopping. I needed a new dress and John needed a new suit. Despite all the plans she had to attend to, Joan found the time to make sure that we were also prepared for her wedding.

Johnny and I had married on the first "Sweetest Day." We always thought that was a good day to be married as our union has lasted 55 years and it is stronger than ever. So, when our daughter set her date for "Valentines Day," we were sure she would have the same luck we have had with romance filling every day of our lives.

Joan's wedding ceremony was held in the morning. She was so beautiful in her white dress and lace veil. Her eyes seemed bluer than I had ever seen them and her smile told the story of her happiness.

After the ceremony, we were all invited to the Oak Brook Hills Resort for lunch. It was marvelous because the families could really enjoy each other with the gathering being of a moderate size.

That same afternoon, Joan and Ben held a reception at Joan's townhouse in Oakbrook. I am positive that everybody who was invited came. They served champagne, cake and sweets. Toasts were given to the happy couple and they cut their wedding cake amid 150 people who had come to honor their day.

Then the couple flew off to New Orleans to spend their honeymoon reveling with the others who had come for Mardi Gras. Mmm, sounds like another coincidence—I went to New Orleans for my honeymoon too!

Joan is back home now and settling into her life as a married woman. Before my stroke, I always had more energy than I needed and was always on the go doing something. Joan is so much like me in that matter.

Most recently she has been going to school to finish her doctorate in education while also teaching at Columbia College. She writes newspaper articles and has a website of her own about yoga. She has also been busy doing publicity tours for the books she has written on yoga, meditation and massage. These books are nationally known and she continually updates them as new information and techniques come to the foreground. When she had time to date, I am not sure, but she also manages to make plenty of time for Ben who puts her first in his life and loves her very much.

People think only the French know how to make crepes...well, who do you think they learned it from?

NALESNIKI
(Polish Crepes)
Ingredients:

3 eggs
3/4 cup milk
2 Tbsp. sugar 1/2 tsp. salt
6 to 8 Tbsp. flour

Beat eggs. Mix sugar, salt and flour well together and stir quickly into the eggs.
Add milk and beat hard.
Have ready one or more heavy six inch crepe pans, lightly buttered and well heated.
Pour just enough batter into each to cover the bottom of the pan when it is tilted and swirled.
Shake the crepes over the fire until they are slightly browned on the bottom and firm to the touch on top. Do not turn. Put them aside to cool.
This may be done several hours before serving.
This recipe makes 16 to 18 crepes.

APPLE FILLING FOR NALESNIKI
(Servings: 4)

2 large tart apples	1/3 cup butter
1/2 tsp. cinnamon	1/3 cup sugar
4 Tbsp. sugar	1/3 cup bread crumbs
1 tsp. lemon juice	

Cook apples with sugar, cinnamon and lemon juice.
Mash apples slightly until it resembles course applesauce. Cool.
Fill crepes and roll up.
Place on buttered baking dish and brush well with melted butter.
Mix sugar with bread crumbs and butter and sprinkle over top.
Bake in 350° F. oven for 20 minutes.

Lifestyle

Wednesday, November 03, 2004   Suburban Life   Page **39**

Budilovsky

John and Leona Budilovsky of Oak Brook, formerly of Westchester, celebrated their 54th wedding anniversary.

Former ballroom dancers, the couple celebrated their anniversary by seeing "Shall We Dance?," a movie about ballroom dancing shot in Chicago, followed by an intimate dinner at Bohemian Crystal Restaurant.

Mr. Budilovsky married the former Leona Turlo Oct. 21, 1950 in Chicago.

They are the founders and former owners of the Westchester Budilovsky Funeral Home from 1957 to 1974. Prior to 1957, they owned Budilovsky Funeral Home in Chicago. Both retired in 1974 and have turned their attention to penning books.

He is the former president of the Westchester Chamber of Commerce, former president and lieutenant governor of Westchester Kiwanis Club, past president of Bohemian National Funeral Directors Association and is currently a member of Athlon Philoi.

She belonged to the Westchester Women's Club and is currently a member of Athlon Philoi.

The couple's children include Joan Budilovsky (Ben Kuzniar) of Oak Brook, author of Yo Joan column, which appears in several editions of Liberty Suburban Chicago Newspapers; Jane Zeck (Richard) of Minneapolis; and the late John Budilovsky, Jr., husband of Lourdes Tizon Budilovsky of Batavia.

Grandchildren include Josephine Budilovsky; and Rebecca and Richard Zeck.

Leona and John Budilovsky

50

I have now been married for 55 years to a wonderful man who I greatly love. I am sure that he loves me too. We've had three children bless our marriage, one son and two daughters. Both our mothers have left us and gone to heaven. They're watching us from heaven so we need to be good, so that they won't be ashamed of us. By now they have joined up with their husbands and our son Bud. I hope that they are all together looking after each other.

Most everyone has a desire to live to a certain age. I thought about the age I'd like to live to and came up with 111. This would give me enough time to clean up my drawers and also finish any unfinished work I had. I hope that coming to this age I'd be able to do all that is needed to be done. I hope that I'll be able to take care of myself until I reach that age too.

I wrote my first book in 1998 before I had my stroke and before my son died. Because life became so topsy-turvy after that, we didn't get it published until the year 2000. My daughter Joan who is a published author arranged for us to have book signings together at various Barnes and Nobles and Borders Bookstores. At my first book signing, everyone from the family came to cheer me on and it became quite a festive event. I was so happy to have everyone together celebrating my mother's life, which was what my first book was about.

Lady Lee was much harder to write, but I was dedicated to getting it finished. I am proud of the work that went into it. After my stroke, I didn't know if I would be able to do many of the things I am now able to do again. It is my hope that this book will give inspiration to other stroke victims to strive to get every ounce of joy out of life and to live it to the fullest.

There is still a great deal I would like to do while I'm still able to do it. I'd like to help my grand-children get a good start in life, in the same way that I helped my son by working in his law office all those years ago. Although I am not as physically agile as I was back then, I'd like to have a huge garage sale to sell all that isn't needed any longer. I'll give the money from the sale to my grandchildren hoping this will help them get started. In fact, I have been doing this at the end of summer for several years now, and plan to keep right on doing this again next summer.

There is so much in the drawers that I no longer use or need and I'll sell it all. I want my drawers to be all clean. I'll also clean the kitchen cabinets and sell whatever I no longer use. I don't want my children to have a great deal of work cleaning out my drawers. I'll do it for them.

As I sit here still living a full life, there are many things I am grateful for like my mother-in-law and the help she gave me when I was first married. Also for my parents who were very protective of me. I am thankful that my mother was a great seamstress who made most of my dresses. But what I am most grateful for is my wonderful husband, Johnny and our children.

Enjoy your young years. They can return back in our minds and thoughts. Every experience, every day, every year shapes the people we encounter and the people we become. Each moment can deepen our love, if we choose this to be. Continue learning and you will always remain young.

It all started when I was young—now, I am older, much older and have learned a great deal about love, life and people. But, even now, I still have so much more I want to see and do. I hope I have enough time in my life to do everything I want to do. It is only now, after living for 83 years that I realize how short life really is. In closing, don't put off until tomorrow what you can do today because tomorrow may never come.

Recipes by Chapter

1. Cheese Rolled Dumplings
2. Old Fashioned Cold Slaw
3. Roast Rabbit
4. Potato Pancakes
5. Ponczki (Bismarks)
6. Praline Cookies
7. Dump Cake
8. Braised Beef Heart
9. Salmon Patties and Halibut Steaks
10. Duck
11. Cream Puffs
12. Sulc
13. Fool Proof Roast Beef Tenderloin and Horse Radish
14. Chicken Dumpling Soup
15. Chocolate-Filled Snowballs
16. Best Ever Brownies and Cream Cheese Kolacky
17. Kuba
18. Cold Beet Soup
19. Lemon Bars
20. Chicken Breast Supreme
21. Nut Balls

22. Tripe Soup

23. Chocolate Chip Cookies

24. Apple Puffed Pancake

25. Pierogi filled with Sauerkraut and Mushrooms

26. Fleecki

27. Buterball Cookies

28. No Pull Apple Strudel

29. Kolacky

30. Grape Kolack and Baked Listy

31. Spaghetti and Hamburger and Chili

32. BBQ Beef

33. Lee' Barley Soup

34. Cabbage Parcels

35. Ptacky (Pigs in Blanket)

36. Potato Chip Cookies

37. Bigos—Hunter Stew

38. Rye Bread

39. Helena's Cabbage Soup & Josephine's Pea Soup

40. Polish Noodles and Cabbage

41. Duck Giblets and Rice

42. Zucchini Bread and Banana Nut Loaf

43. Stuffed Green Peppers

44. Sesame Veal Cutlets and Spinach

45. Chicken Paprikash

46. Kasha

47. Fruit Coffee Cake

48. Dressing and Liver & Onions

49. Cheesecake Cookies

50. Nalesniki

Our wedding portrait taken in October, 1950

And, still dancing after all these years.

0-595-33361-3

Printed in the United States
24719LVS00004BA/150